Finding Top Talent

How to Search for Leaders in Academic Medicine

William T. Mallon, Ed.D., R. Kevin Grigsby, D.S.W., and Mary Dupont Barrett

with the research assistance of April Corrice

Published by

Association of American Medical Colleges

Washington, D.C.

Library of Congress Cataloging-in-Publication Data

Mallon, William T. (William Thomas), 1969-
    Finding top talent : how to search for leaders in academic medicine / William T. Mallon, R. Kevin Grigsby, and Mary Dupont Barrett ; with the research assistance of April Corrice.
        p. ; cm.
    Includes bibliographical references and index.
    Summary: "A resource on how to conduct the recruitment process for administrative leaders in medical schools and teaching hospitals"—Provided by publisher.
    ISBN 978-1-57754-087-8 (alk. paper)
    1. Medical teaching personnel—Selection and appointment—United States I. Grigsby, R. Kevin. II. Barrett, Mary Dupont. III. Association of American Medical Colleges. IV. Title.
    [DNLM: 1. Academic Medical Centers—manpower—Handbooks. 2. Academic Medical Centers—organization & administration—Handbooks. 3. Leadership—Handbooks. 4. Personnel Selection—methods—Handbooks.]
    R745.M326 2009
    610.71'173—dc22
                                                                2009034591

Available from
Association of American Medical Colleges
Section for Publication Orders
2450 N Street N.W., Washington, D.C. 20037-1134
Phone: (202) 828-0416   Fax: (202) 828-1123
www.aamc.org/publications

Table of Contents

Acknowledgments

We would like to acknowledge the AAMC's previous publication, *The Successful Medical School Department Chair, Module 1: Search, Selection, Appointment, Transition* (2002), upon which this current work is based. Julien Biebuyck, M.D., was the guiding force behind the *Successful Chair* series and provided a wonderful platform from which to create this updated and expanded handbook.

We benefitted immensely from the superior assistance of April Corrice. She authored the August 2009 *Analysis in Brief* on unconscious bias that informs chapter 5, played a major role in the research (Mallon & Corrice, 2009) that undergirds particular chapters, assisted with references, and superbly edited the manuscript.

A portion of chapter 4 is based upon a previously published article in *Academic Medicine*. We gratefully acknowledge the coauthors on the original: Darrell Kirch, David Hefner, and Chip Souba.

We also wish to acknowledge the great support, insight, and advice of the AAMC's Leadership Search and Recruitment Advisory Committee. This group generously reviewed an earlier version of this handbook, and provided insight to make it stronger. We, not they, are responsible for errors, omissions, and inaccuracies. Members of this group include:

- **Steven M. Block, M.B.B.Ch.**, Senior Associate Dean and Professor of Pediatrics at Wake Forest University School of Medicine
- **Elizabeth Bolt**, Associate Dean for Administration, University of Wisconsin School of Medicine and Public Health
- **Peter F. Buckley, M.D.**, Associate Dean for Leadership Development and Chair, Department of Psychiatry and Health Behavior, Medical College of Georgia School of Medicine
- **Tammy D. Jamison**, Director, Physician and Executive Recruiting, Lehigh Valley Hospital and Health Network
- **Kathleen Ruff**, Chief of Staff, Office of the President and Dean, College of Medicine, Northeast Ohio Universities College of Medicine
- **Rebecca Trumbull**, Executive Director, Education, Northwestern University Feinberg School of Medicine
- **Anne L. Wright, Ph.D.**, Associate Dean for Faculty Affairs and Research Professor, Arizona Respiratory Center and Department of Pediatrics, University of Arizona College of Medicine

Finally, we wish to acknowledge the medical schools and teaching hospitals that generously granted permission to reproduce documents and materials: Lehigh Valley Health Network, Medical College of Georgia School of Medicine, Northeastern Ohio Universities College of Medicine, Stanford University School of Medicine, University of Arizona College of Medicine, University of South Florida College of Medicine, and University of Wisconsin School of Medicine and Public Health.

A note about the terminology in this publication

This book is about the leadership search and recruiting process in academic medical centers. *The Successful Medical School Department Chair* (Biebuyck & Mallon, 2002) specifically focused on the hiring process for department chairs. In *Finding Top Talent*, we broaden the leadership search process to include other critical roles in medical schools and teaching hospitals, such as center directors, vice/associate deans, and others.

Throughout *Finding Top Talent*, we refer to the hiring or appointing authority (that is, the person who makes the decision about whom to hire) as the dean or CEO, but recognize that the individual who has hiring authority may be a senior vice president, chancellor, or other senior executive, or that authority may be shared. To avoid unnecessary and repetitive definitions and explanations, we have used "dean" or "CEO" throughout the text. Readers should substitute the governance terms appropriate to their own specific institutions.

1 The Ten "C's" of Searching

Chapter Digest

The premise of this book is that process is the key to every successful search. *The Ten "C's" of Searching* are characteristics evident when medical schools and teaching hospitals search well:

1. Continuity
2. Communication
3. The Charge
4. Culture
5. Candidates (and their competence)
6. The Chair
7. Composition
8. Conduct
9. Confidentiality
10. Closure
(See pages 2–4.)

How well do medical schools and teaching hospitals search for new leaders? Why does it take such a long time to find the right person for a position? Why do we read as often as we do about botched searches and leadership failures?

And what can we do about it?

The premise of this book is that **process is THE key to every successful search**. That process by which leaders are identified for important roles in medical schools and teaching hospitals—deans, CEOs, department chairs, center directors, and other major administrative positions—is "in major disarray" (Creasman, 2001). Why the disarray? Because "most search committees are ill-equipped or unwilling to undertake the labor intensive process required to truly search" for new leaders (Grigsby et al., 2004).

Why are recruitment searches in academic medicine such a source of complaint and consternation? This isn't a new question, and the responses aren't new problems.

"Process is the key to every successful search."

The Problems

Based on extensive research with executive search consultants and medical school deans and administrators, the criticism of the process can be distilled in several overarching themes.

1. Pre-Work

The traditional academic search process does not sufficiently address *in advance of the search getting underway* the characteristics, skill sets, and competencies the new leader is expected to have. Often, institutions don't think in outcome terms: specifically, in one or two years, what evidence would demonstrate whether you have hired the right person? What would be different? What should have improved? What should have been started and what stopped? Once those hoped-for circumstances have been clearly defined, so, too, will the competencies or expertise that candidates need to achieve those outcomes.

2. Committees

A committee approach to the search process honors academic traditions but can also impede outcomes. Some schools are saddled with arcane requirements about who is required to be on the committee—polices that may not reflect the complex health care enterprise in which academic medical centers operate. In other cases, committees simply can be too large. In either case, the result is often that the committee is not populated with people sufficiently committed to the search process.

3. The "Charge"

When search committees are used, the charge by the hiring authority to that group—that is, the specific skills and requirements for the position as outlined in Problem 1 (Pre-Work)—can be a source of friction. In some cases, the goals and expectations of the dean or CEO may diverge from the direction the department or unit has taken. The committee members hear the charge but might not listen to it, either because they are not clear about the dean's vision, or because the committee thinks of itself as a *selection* rather than a *search* committee.

4. Casting the Net

"Far too often, the search process is passive and can appear closed."

Committees can be under the delusion of "advertise it and they will come." Several ads in prominent journals or newsletters plus a handful of letters to peers around the country might only work in the most prestigious of positions, and maybe not even then. Far too often, the search process is passive and can appear closed. Highly qualified leaders may not apply if it appears that finalists have been predetermined.

5. Scheduling

Scheduling committee meetings and candidate interviews can take forever. Instead of maintaining momentum, an extended search gets bogged down and candidates lose interest—and may even accept less attractive offers at other institutions because the process is too slow.

6. Confidentiality

In some searches, confidentiality is not respected. Committee members might conduct a parallel search process—contacting colleagues at a candidate's current institution and gathering information (or worse, gossip) on the side. Such behavior is damaging to everyone—candidates, search committee, and institution. This behavior might be another factor in seriously limiting the pool of interested and highly qualified candidates who do not believe their privacy will be respected.

7. Professionalism

Overall, the search process isn't conducted with the same high degree of professionalism that is routinely afforded to and expected in education, clinical care, and research endeavors in the academic medical center.

This handbook will explore these deficiencies in depth and offer solutions to overcome them.

The Ten "C's" of Searching

What makes for a well-crafted and executed search? The AAMC's Leadership Search Advisory Committee identified the following 10 characteristics evident when medical schools and teaching hospitals search well. We believe they are interdependent in priority; the organization's leaders must attend to all components to effect a positive search.

☐ **Continuity**. While the fundamentals of how to run any one search are important—and will be discussed at length throughout this handbook—a critical element of overall success for the institution is in the *system* of searching; that is, the continuity from one search to the next.

Are searches run with a common framework and approach? Are searches staffed in the same manner? Is there an institutional point person or team who ensures consistency and quality control in the mechanics of the search? If you were a fly on the wall in two separate searches, would you observe the same type of conduct from the search committee members and adherence to the same values?

More and more institutional executives view the search function as an organization-wide system that enables the integration of one's leadership team with institutional culture.

☐ **Communication.** Communication in any organizational system is important, of course, but is multilayered for leadership searches, easily creating bottlenecks and confusion. Communication must be open and timely between the dean/CEO and the search committee, the dean/CEO and her or his staff, the search chair and committee, the committee and the candidates, and the committee and interview panels.

☐ **Charge.** The charge from the hiring authority to the search committee is, in effect, a prescription of needed competencies and skill sets for the position. The charge needs to describe up front what attributes will bring success (preferably defined in outcome terms). This kind of pre-work enables the search chair and committee members to understand and embrace the future plans for the department or unit and promotes the ability to focus attention on formulating interview questions that directly address "fit."

☐ **Culture.** According to Schein (2004), organizational culture consists of the basic assumptions about the world shared by a group of people that determine their perceptions, feelings, and behavior. In high-functioning search processes, organizational leaders and the search committee are aware of the different layers of culture: at the institutional and unit levels and sub-cultures therein. Search committee members strive to find a "fit" between organizational culture and values and the leader's style and preferences.

"Despite differences among sub-cultures within an academic medical center, the fundamentals of the search process should be consistent across the organization."

We made two core assumptions: First, the search criteria for each position will be unique and specific to the department or unit. Second, despite differences among sub-cultures within an academic medical center (e.g., among different academic departments), the fundamentals of the search process should be consistent across the organization.

☐ **Candidates (and their Competence).** All search committees and institutional leaders envision scores of superior candidates clamoring to join the organization. In high-functioning searches, the candidate pool is spot-on because of the outstanding legwork and preparation that the organization has done prior to the search being launched—through careful consideration of the characteristics and competencies needed for success in the position. More and more institutions recognize that candidates are best evaluated for their fit for the leadership challenges of the position, not for the weight of their CV. It is important that the committee develop standards or indicators for the level of performance and behavior that meet the demands of the institution's plan for the new leader, and satisfy the dean's charge to the group.

☐ **Chair.** The search committee chair (if there is a search committee—more on this later) is a key institutional leadership role. Search chairs must be thoughtfully appointed, provided with adequate administrative support, given appropriate training, and held accountable for leading a highly professional search. The key word is "lead." Search chairs are vital institutional leaders.

☐ **Composition**. Many individuals participate in the search process for institutional leaders, and their selection needs thoughtful consideration. Choosing who serves on the search committee should not be rote decision or one left to anachronistic policy dictums. Who will interview candidates, and why have they been selected to do so? Are these the right people? Will they and can they act as both interviewers and recruiters? Do the search committee and interview panels represent broad and deep diversity of perspectives, backgrounds, and levels within the organization? Can committee members respectfully but strongly present differing opinions while seeking consensus?

"In addition to identifying the best candidates for a position, search committees also must be recruitment teams."

☐ **Conduct**. Conduct is both a noun and verb. As a noun, conduct refers to the behavior of those involved in the search process. In addition to identifying the best candidates for a position, search committees also must be recruitment teams. As a verb, conduct refers to process—how the search process is handled. Principles of good conduct in the search process should include transparency, confidentiality, and integrity.

☐ **Confidentiality** is maintained in searches that work well. Breaches of confidentiality undermine the integrity of the search and hurt all parties— candidates, the search committee, institutional leaders, and the unit for which a new leader is being sought. Some argue that confidentiality is at odds with academic values of openness. We do not believe that confidentiality and opaqueness are synonyms. Confidentiality, ultimately, is about respect for both the people and the process.

When searching for the best of all possible candidates, remember that the pool is likely to be small, and that those people you hope to attract may be colleagues or friends who have occasion to compare notes! In all searches, candidates must have legally protected rights to privacy and fairness, which could be compromised by conversations not authorized by the committee.

☐ **Closure**. A search is not over when the search committee forwards its finalist list to the dean, or when the dean selects a new leader, or when the new leader accepts the offer and a public announcement is made. Organizations must attend to "on-boarding" and the successful integration of the leader into the life of the institution, as well as the respectful and gracious interaction with candidates who are not chosen for the position.

Equally important is an openness of the organization to the change in leadership. Particularly difficult roadblocks and resistance can emerge if the unit must change the direction or principal structure. Search committee members can do a great deal of work as "ambassadors" in this regard once the selection is complete.

These ten "C's" of searching will serve as the scaffolding for the remainder of this handbook. In subsequent chapters, you will learn about best practices and innovative ideas for preparations and pre-search activities, the composition and charge of the search committee, candidate attributes and skill sets, overcoming unconscious biases, search strategies, candidate evaluation, "concierge-level" service, negotiating and making the offer, and welcoming new leaders into the organization.

2 Preparations

At the time of an opening for a department chair, center director, or other leadership position, the first step for the institution and its leaders is not to act, but to reflect. This is a particularly difficult task when the departure is unexpected or where there have been problems with the incumbent leader. If the institution needs new direction, clarity of purpose, and stability, the dean or CEO will be challenged by the clamor for immediate action and quick solutions. And while it is vital that action be visible and communication be quick and clear, the critical imperative at this time is contemplation and analysis. Where are the institution and the particular unit heading, and what characteristics and competencies are essential in a new leader to help the institution and unit get there?

Organization and Position Assessment

Marchese and Lawrence (2006) rightly describe a vacancy as an "organizational opportunity." They point out that the organization has the occasion to (1) revisit the function, roles, and goals of the past, and (2) reconsider the type of person needed to achieve these goals in the future. In order to achieve the best appointment, the first step for institutional leaders is not the appointment of a search committee but a "process of thought" (Marchese & Lawrence, 2006, p.1).

Typically, however, medical schools and teaching hospitals do not pay adequate attention to the front-end of the process. Organizational leaders (and search committee chairs) must remember that this organizational assessment *is* the beginning of the search process; it is a leadership function, not a search committee function (although in some cases, the search committee may have a role in its execution).

Important questions to ask during this assessment phase include:
- Should this department/division/center/unit continue to exist in its present form?
- What evidence in 1-3 years will convince you that this department/division/center/unit has been successful?
- What is the organization trying to achieve, and how does this role get you there?
- What problem is this role helping to solve for the organization?
- What are the three most important outcomes you want this new recruit to achieve in his or her first three years?

Too often, the leadership search tends to be a reaction to the past rather than being viewed as an opportunity to improve performance and outcome by investing in the future. The typical assessment process isn't rigorous; often a vision is not articulated. The major tasks and challenges of the department are never put in writing. The

Chapter Digest

The first step is not to act but to reflect.

* Think in outcome terms: what are the three most important outcomes you want this new leader to achieve in her or his first three years? (See below.)
* Prior to starting the search, conduct a review of the department, center, program, or unit internally or externally. (See pages 6–8.)
* Use an interim position to give an internal candidate a trial run. These positions can open the door to minority and female candidates who might otherwise be overlooked. (See page 10.)

organization and its leaders don't take the time and effort to critically evaluate the skills needed to fulfill those tasks. Complicating the matter, many positions in academic medical centers are complex. Positions such as center directors and chief medical officers can be new and ill-defined.

Moreover, leadership posts traditionally have not focused on leadership abilities. For example, department chairs (especially clinical chairs) have been hired based on success in research (and publication) and program building. Inherent in building a program are leadership skills: managing budgets, recruiting and retaining talent, etc. But there has not been an explicit focus on leadership skills, especially the ability to create, develop, and manage broad-based strategic relationships. In the best departments, chairs have these competencies, but perhaps despite the search process, not because of it.

"There has not been an explicit focus on leadership skills, especially the ability to create, develop, and manage broad-based strategic relationships."

Interdisciplinary centers are changing that traditional model. Because of the current environment that demands collaboration and team work, more department chairs are "getting it," but not necessarily because of a purposeful change in the recruitment process.

In the absence of clear definitions of outcomes and the leadership skills that will achieve those outcomes, the search committee will focus on what they know best: academic abilities, not leadership skills.

For Departments: Review of Discipline and Departmental Mission

As part of the organizational assessment, institutional leaders may wish to conduct a thorough analysis of the department and discipline itself. A department review is, in part, an environmental analysis. Where does the department stand vis-à-vis its competitors and collaborators on key mission areas? What is the future of the department and discipline over the next 5-10 years? What is the national environment for the discipline, department, or specialty? A high-quality review is not a departmental "report card." Rather, the review uses the data generated during the past to inform the future. Information about the future trajectory of the department is critical for the search committee and its chair as they engage in the search process.

There are various ways in which a dean or CEO may assess the status of a department, center, or program when its leader departs. In the course of our work, we identified a number of models, which tend to differ in two dimensions. The first model is *who* conducts the review—external consultant from the discipline, the search consultant, the search chair, or even the department itself? The second model is degree of formality of the review—some schools have traditions of formal review processes with well-defined criteria; in other cases, the review can be quick but provide less in-depth analysis.

Internal Reviews
- *Formal Departmental Review*
  For those institutions with a formally structured departmental review process, it can be a simple matter to include the practice of a mandatory review of the department whenever its leadership changes. While this comprehensive review might be appropriate in some circumstances (especially if none has been done in many years), it will not be the right course for all. Those institutions already

managing through significant change (such as the on-boarding of a new dean or CEO) may have less impetus for a formal review and analysis.

- *Search Committee Review*

Some deans combine the initial stages of the search with a departmental review by charging the search committee with the review. In this approach, the search committee has an advantage of getting a true "feel" of problems and challenges.

Stanford University School of Medicine, for example, uses a framework of meetings with a variety of people to ensure that the committee members understand the departmental and institutional needs and priorities.

**Stanford University School of Medicine
Search Committee Guidelines**

The search committee must...
- Understand the department and school perspective
    - o Meet with appropriate individuals within and outside the department
        - To understand the department from a variety of perspectives—clinical, research, education, administration
    - o Meet with the dean
        - To understand the qualities sought in a future leader of the department in the context of the department and the school
- Develop objective criteria for the position
- Understand broader school and institutional priorities
    - o Meet with the dean and senior associate dean for diversity and leadership
        - To understand the focused efforts required to meet diversity goals of the school
        - To understand the role of the diversity advocate
        - To understand the resources available to the committee
- Understand the role and expectations of the search committee
- Meet with the dean
        - To understand the rigor expected of the search process
        - To understand the role and expectations of the search committee

PRODUCT: A solid understanding of the department, the priorities of the school, and the desired qualifications for the candidates, to enable the search committee to proceed with clear direction and conduct its work effectively

- *Search Chair Review*

The chair of the search committee can conduct the review, seeking input and information from the current leader, departmental faculty, and others with a stake in the department's future planning. Having the search chair perform the review dovetails with her or his responsibilities, as the chair must understand both the "what" and the "who" of the search. Once armed with information from the departmental review, the search chair can then articulate the nature of the "who" —who would make the most appropriate candidate for the position.

A limitation with this approach is that the evaluation process might be construed as a way of lengthening the search process itself or appearing to give the chair more responsibility than institutional leaders feel is warranted.

- *Internal Department "Audit"*
In the absence of a formal process of departmental review, the dean's office may opt for an informally conducted, but comprehensively managed, internal audit. In this case, the department could be required to provide baseline data, including program evaluations, research in progress, operational budget status, funding or grants pending, and so on. The dean and relevant leaders would meet to discuss and share observations, and the dean's office, perhaps in partnership with the CEO, COO, and/or director of the hospital or medical center, would evaluate and determine future direction for the department and its new leader.

External Reviews
- *Search Consultant Assessment*
When search consultants are engaged to help with recruitments, most will initiate a departmental review in preparing the position analysis. In fact, many search consultants insist on conducting in-depth interviews with stakeholders throughout the organization before embarking on any other aspects of a search process.

- *External Consultant Review*
A department review can be done by external consultants, whose expertise and presumed objectivity could provide the necessary justification for the dean or CEO to advance more substantial changes to the department or major adjustments to its future objectives. This option may be the least attractive to faculty in some departments if they fear that outsiders cannot know the environment, political considerations, or operational culture of the department, and, therefore, whose trust level may be low.

Whatever the process or practice, it is crucial that the state of the department be analyzed before a working role definition for the new leader can be considered. Those responsible for its conduct should make every effort to be open and forthright about the priorities and objectives of the dean and/or CEO, be clear and candid about the process, and be ready to explain (or perhaps to defend) the conclusions to those who will help lead the department forward.

Do You Need to Search? Should You Use a Search Committee?

Much of the remainder of this handbook has two assumptions: (1) a search process will occur, and (2) leaders will delegate that task to a search committee. But neither should be assumed from the get-go. Rather, senior leadership of the organization should make a conscious decision about both.

Do You Need to Search?
Medical schools and teaching hospital should have robust plans for succession for their senior leadership positions. While succession planning and talent development may be variable across academic medicine, sometimes the department, center, or unit has identified a future leader ready to assume the position. If that is the case, why search? If you already have the talent ready at the door, why go through the process (and expend the time and money) of a national search?

You might consider at least three reasons to conduct a national search, even if there is an internal candidate who appears to be well prepared, who has been groomed for the position, and who may be serving in an interim role:

- To "act affirmatively" to ensure the entire range of candidates is explored. There may be highly qualified women or persons from underrepresented minorities who may be well suited and/or better qualified than an internal candidate. A reasonable process should truly "search" for the best, most qualified candidates. Assuming that the internal candidate is the most qualified may cause committees to overlook more qualified candidates, especially if those candidates are not viewed as one of "the usual suspects."

- To validate the internal candidate as being truly viable in the search process. Otherwise, the individual may be treated as an "heir apparent" who gets the job as a function of cronyism or ethnocentric bias.

- To glean important information from external candidates who view your organization from a different perspective. This is an optimal time to ask others about their observations of the organization as a means of testing the validity of your own perception.

Should You Use a Search Committee?
Search committees are the norm at most medical schools for administrative leadership positions, perhaps less frequently used for leadership posts in teaching hospitals. Before it is assumed that the search committee is the best way to handle leadership recruitment, we might consider its advantages, limitations, and innovations.

Search committees emerge from academic culture and tradition ("how we do things here") and, less frequently, by policy mandate. As Marchese and Lawrence (2006) remind us, search committees are a relatively new phenomenon in the long history of academe. At their best, search committees allow participation and voice and invite differing perspectives. Research on diversity and teams tells us that broad representation and collaborative efforts lead to improved organizational outcomes.

Search committees are also subject to legitimate criticisms. Some members may be placed on the committee because of arcane requirements of committee composition rather than because of the competencies they bring. Committees can be inefficient, become embroiled in infighting, or get bogged down. Committees may not allow or accommodate creative thinking that identifies "break-through" candidates.

Despite their limitations, many medical schools and teaching hospital use search committees because of substantive benefits as well as academic norms. But deans and CEOs may wish to consider new ways of conceiving that traditional model. See chapter 3 for ideas.

The Use of Interims

At times, it may be imperative for the institution's stability and operational effectiveness to appoint a leader for an interim period. There are advantages and disadvantages to this temporary appointment.

The terms *interim* and *acting* are sometimes used synonymously. However, there is a difference:

- An "interim" serves as the head of a unit while a search is conducted to find a new permanent leader. There is a clear expectation that the previous leader who had occupied the position will not return.
- An individual in an "acting" role serves as the leader while the permanent leader experiences a temporary absence—but anticipates returning. No matter the purpose of the period of leave, there is a clear expectation that the leader will return to the position (Quillen, Aber, & Grigsby, in press).

There may be many reasons for using an interim to fill a position:

- To give an internal candidate a trial run
- To allow healing or to "clean up a mess" after a traumatic situation or fresh turmoil
- After an involuntary separation, resignation, or death
- When there is ambivalence about doing a search for a replacement. For example, do we need to recruit for this position now? What is the future of this department?

An important question to consider is what type of person is best suited to be an interim: someone who is interested in becoming the permanent leader or someone who is definitely *not* interested? The dean and other leaders must be clear about the reasons for and expectation of an interim appointment. Preparing such messages before the announcement of an interim appointment eases tension and helps tamp down gossip and speculation.

Interim leadership can be an opportunity
Appointment of interim leadership while a search is conducted can "open the door" to minority and female candidates who might otherwise be overlooked. In many searches, the pool of underrepresented minority and female candidates may not be robust. A period of mentorship followed by an interim leadership experience can help to prepare persons to serve as full-time leaders. This strategy offers a promising approach to increasing the pool of talented female and minority candidates for leadership positions.

3 The Search Committee: Composition and Charge

Chapter Digest

* Can search committee members adapt an institutional mindset? Search committees are evolving from representative-based to competency-based. (See pages 11–12.)
* The core search committee. Some organizations have search committees comprised of a core group of senior leaders or co-chaired by the same individual. (See page 14.)
* Professionalizing the search. The search and recruitment function can be best served when core dedicated professionals or teams support all leadership search processes. (See page 16.)

There are two broad functions within any search for a new leader. The search committee has purview over one, but not over the other:

* *Searching and screening* are the responsibilities of the committee appointed by, and advisory to, the dean, CEO, or hiring authority. Searching involves "casting the net" as widely as possible—nationally and possibly internationally—to identify a candidate pool. While the committee coordinates the call for nominees and applicants, all members of the academic community are invited to participate in this stage. Second, members of the search committee conduct the screening process in confidence. Screening involves the evaluation of the applicants to reduce the number to a list of *at least two* final candidates submitted to the dean. Forwarding the name of one candidate is tantamount to selecting the new leader. Selection and hiring is beyond the purview of the search committee.

* *Selecting* the new institutional leader—department chair, institute director, vice dean, etc.—is the primary responsibility of the dean, CEO, or hiring authority. In the traditional medical school setting, the "selection process" refers to the stage that commences when the search committee sends the list of finalists to the dean. For leadership positions with clinical responsibilities, the teaching hospital CEO may have a formal role or may provide critical input, depending on the structure and relationships between medical school and hospital. The dean may also seek advice and input from trusted academic and clinical leaders. The dean makes personal phone calls to references both "on-list" and "off-list" (i.e., respected national leaders) and in some cases may conduct reverse site visits to the candidate's current institution.

The dean or CEO and the search committee chair must ensure that the search committee understands its responsibility and limitations. The committee cannot usurp the selection function by either ranking the finalists or submitting only one candidate as finalist. Most deans instruct the committee to submit a specified number of final candidates in alphabetical—rather than rank—order.

Who Should be Included on the Search Committee?

Recent trends in the composition of search committees—like the composition of the most effective governing boards—suggest that search committees are evolving from representative-based to competency-based. In other words, members of the search committee are selected for their talents and skills to identify the right candidate, and not based on the constituency each committee member represents.

To identify the "right" candidate, members of the committee must have a good understanding of the special nature of the institution and the department, center, or

> *"Search committees are evolving from representative-based to competency-based."*

functional unit that the leader will direct. They also must know the attributes and skill sets required to be successful in the specific role.

"The members of the search committee also function as recruiters of the best candidates."

Committee members should be good judges of people. The members of the search committee also function as recruiters of the best candidates. McLauglin and Riesman (1990) stress that "searches involve courtship quite as much as they involve selection" (p. 59). Marchese and Lawrence (2006) warn those leaders who appoint members to the search committee to "avoid the appointment of known cranks, gossips, and egotists" (p. 7). Committee members must understand how to build consensus and how to compromise.

For department chair searches, obvious constituencies include other department chairs, faculty members, hospital administrators, nurses, medical residents and fellows, medical students, and, in the case of a basic science chair search, graduate students. Many medical schools include community members (both community physicians as well as lay individuals) and other internal and external "customers" of the unit.

Research has indicated that including the "customers" or "end-users" of the department's services (educational, research, clinical, or community-based) may lead to better outcomes. For example, one study found that while customers are included on search committees only 7 percent of the time, in those cases the selection outcome was successful 70 percent of the time, compared to a 45 percent success rate in searches where these perspectives were not included (Sessa & Taylor, 2000).

A key consideration in selecting individuals for a search committee is whether they can be candid, set aside political agendas, handle conflict like adults, and listen well before making decisions (Sessa & Taylor, 2000). Committee members must adapt an institutional mindset, not a unit-level view of the organization. Garrison (1989) warns institutions to be careful of placing individuals on the search committee to eliminate their chances of becoming a candidate. Such individuals can start "waging guerilla warfare" on other candidates and might conduct selective reference checks without the permission of the committee chair (p. 25). Needless to say, these reference checks tend to point out the weaknesses of the other candidates without an appropriate balance on their appropriate strengths.

Important Initial Steps in the Development of a Search Committee

- The **selection of the chair** of the search committee. The search committee chair becomes an important advisor to the dean, CEO, or hiring authority, not only during crucial stages of the search process but, importantly, during the recruitment process of the leading candidate and during the transition period when the new hire arrives. This advisory role is most readily and effectively performed in an atmosphere of mutual trust and respect.

- The appointment of the search committee by the dean or by the dean and the search committee chair.

- The balanced composition of the membership of the search committee. Individual institutions may have different guidelines or policies that address certain mandated representation on these committees, although current practice suggests a shift away from mandated representation toward competency-based selection. Each institution may also have a tradition or policy concerning the representation of the department in question on the committee. See below for more information about departmental representation on the search committee.

Representation of the Home Department on the Search Committee
For department chair searches, representation from the home department on the search committee is a controversial issue that varies from school to school. By tradition, some schools have one representative from the home department; others have several; and some do not allow any representatives from the home department to serve.

A departmental representative may be included on the search committee to inform and educate the committee about the national and local challenges faced by the discipline, the honor societies and leading academic journals of the discipline, and the specific leadership characteristics needed by that particular department at that particular time.

Unfortunately, department representatives sometimes see their role to serve as a conduit of confidential search committee information back to the department. Because of this potential confidentiality breach, some institutions have a policy of *no* departmental representation on the search committee.

Given the potential downsides of departmental representation on the committee itself, deans and committee chairs may wish to consider whether the committee can be informed and educated about the department's local and national context through alternative methods. For example, some schools appoint a faculty member or chair from a related discipline who knows the department's needs well. Additionally, the committee can and should take the time to meet with faculty members, students, residents and fellows, and clinical staff of the department.

"The search committee chair becomes an important advisor to the dean, CEO, or hiring authority."

Innovations at Work

The Core Search Committee

Using a committee of faculty, administrators, students, fellows, residents, clinical staff, members of the community, and others is a part of the academic culture—in contrast to many other industries that do not use committees at all. While the committee model of searching has advantages, it also has limitations. One major disadvantage is that, traditionally, each search committee in a medical school is formed *de novo*. Each must start from the beginning in learning to work with each other, understanding its role, and running an effective search.

With its core search committee model, the Medical College of Georgia has instituted an innovative search committee model that attempts to keep its strengths—i.e., participation from a cross-section of stakeholders, which brings in a variety of perspectives—and ameliorate its limitations. Each search committee for a new department chair is co-chaired by the same individual—an associate dean for leadership development. This individual carries forward the learning from successful strategies from the previous searches, so each new committee doesn't start from scratch. See Appendix 1 for the position description of the Medical College of Georgia associate dean for leadership development.

Additionally, MCG has created an administrative structure called the Core Operations Administrative Team for Searches (COATS) to coordinate operational details for the search committee. COATS also facilitates the institution's capacity to conduct several executive searches simultaneously. In addition, COATS provides consultation to other institutional searches with a goal of disseminating "best practices," recruitment support (e.g. centralized, secure website), and materials (e.g. local brochures, sample draft letters for candidates).

Focused Search Committee

Another model is a focused search committee, consisting of a limited number of members—a practice used by the University of South Florida. In this case, two individuals external to the organization serve on the search committee (who are paid an honorarium for their time), complementing a small cadre of thought leaders within the organization. This smaller group allows tighter turn-around times, while the external perspectives ensure objectivity.

The composition of such a search committee can convey important messages to the internal community and to candidates. When the University of South Florida was searching for a vice dean of education for its college of medicine, an important focus of the position was interprofessional education across health science colleges. The chair of the search committee was the dean of public health, which reinforced the commitment of interdisciplinary leadership to candidates.

The Chair of the Search Committee

The search committee chair is among the most important leadership roles within the academic medical center. Indeed, who is selected to be chair of the search can greatly influence who is ultimately selected for the position—the quality of the first affects the quality of the second. Yet the importance of the role is often overlooked. In some cases, the search committee elects the chair from among its ranks. We believe the position of search chair should not be determined by election—the outcome is too

> *"The search committee chair is among the most important leadership roles within the academic medical center."*

important. It is a major leadership role. As such, the hiring officer must appoint the chair.

Who should be the chair? Often, it is assumed that the chair of the committee should serve in a comparable role to that position being sought; e.g., a current department chair for chair searches or a major center director or head of a research program for center and institute directors. Sometimes the search chair emerges from university tradition or policy provisions.

Selecting a peer as the search committee chair can be beneficial because that person then knows the nuance of the position. But it should not be assumed that the chair needs to be in a like position. For example, appointing a respected thought leader who is not a department chair may be more effective if the current department chairs don't model the attributes you seek in the new chair.

> *"We believe that academic medical centers must professionalize and centralize the search process for leadership recruitment."*

Skills and attributes of a search committee chair

Leadership Abilities
- Models leadership attributes needed in position
- Understands and can communicate institutional vision, goals, and strategy
- Has the stature to command the respect of the search committee and the department/center/division/unit, and also to demonstrate independence from the hiring authority
- Has no personal agenda
- Is external to the department/center/division/unit
- Can speak on behalf of the dean or CEO, but knows when to and when not to
- Is attuned to issues of organizational culture and management

Organizational Abilities
- Has the time to run an effective search, and manages time well
- Is organized and detail-oriented
- Understands the importance of *process* in the search process

Emotional Intelligence and Personal Attributes
- Is open to learning her or his role
- Can empower the committee by fostering dialogue, managing conflict, soliciting input, and delegating
- Is patient, persistent, and not easily frustrated
- Remains trustworthy and discreet
- Is assertive
- Is articulate and persuasive

Professionalizing the Search: Administrative and Operational Support

We believe that academic medical centers must professionalize and centralize the search process for leadership recruitment. We are not suggesting that medical schools and teaching hospitals necessarily should hire professional search firms (that option is discussed on pp. 35–38.) Rather, we assert that the search and recruitment function is best served when an individual or team supports all leadership search processes.

Many medical schools have moved in this direction. In fact, data gathering by the AAMC in 2008 identified one-third of schools with this centralized function. Medical schools and teaching hospitals employ at least three different models to provide leadership, guidance, and experienced professional administrative support.

"An in-house search consultant is a key advisor to the dean or CEO and to the search committee chair."

- **"In-house" search expert**
  Many medical schools have tapped a seasonal professional to serve as an "in-house" search expert. While this person may oversee the administrative details of the search, her or his role is more complex. An in-house search consultant is a key advisor to the dean or CEO and to the search committee chair. These individuals drive the process and keep the search moving forward. They may offer insight about who could be tapped to serve on the committee, offer advice and tools to ensure that the search is effective and timely, and provide "concierge-level" service to candidates, ensuring the process focuses on recruitment as well as searching. In-house search experts typically attend all search committee meetings as active participants, though they tend not to have voting rights or a formal decision-making role.

  We have observed this role to be filled by professionals with expertise in institutional planning, faculty affairs, and human resources. In some organizations, the chief of staff or vice dean plays this role.

- **Centralized search administrative support**
  Medical schools may also have an administrative support professional who staffs all searches for leadership positions. (This role may be in addition to the in-house search expert described above.) This role provides the crucial administrative and operational support that ensures the process goes smoothly and effectively. Individuals in these roles handle all the logistical details for the search chair and committee: scheduling search committee meetings and coordinating calendars, tracking inquiries and maintaining the search database, ensuring timely communication with applicants and candidates, scheduling travel, and escorting candidates during interviews. This person may coordinate the concierge services during candidate interviews; e.g., meeting candidates at the airport, arranging transportation, identifying local resources of interest (housing, schools, faith communities, hobbies, and cultural interests).

  At some schools, this role is one component of an administrative professional's portfolio—for example, the dean's assistant may also handle these details. But for an academic medical center that conducts many searches each year, the demands might require a dedicated professional, and some institutions have moved in that direction, with titles such as "coordinator of executive searches" and "recruitment coordinator."

- **In-house staffing model**
  A third approach to providing administrative and operational support for the search process is a full-service recruitment office. Many teaching hospitals have offices of physician recruitment. In some cases, the physician recruitment office has also taken responsibility for coordinating leadership-level recruitment as well. Such an arrangement can be very beneficial since these divisions have search competencies. In our experience, though, the enterprise must be large enough to

support a broader recruitment function to justify the resources. For academic medical centers that handle hundreds of physician recruitments each year, an "in-house search firm" might make great sense. Smaller medical schools that don't directly hire physicians are unlikely to choose this route.

In summary, we believe medical schools should appoint a dedicated individual or team to deal with all leadership searches and recruitment. These vital functions involve similar goals and require similar talents, such as planning and successfully organizing campus visits by finalist candidates. It should not be necessary—as it so often is—to "reinvent the wheel" as each search committee begins its task.

"It should not be necessary—as it so often is—to reinvent the wheel as each search committee begins its task."

Important qualities for administrative support professionals who provide the essential infrastructure to search processes

- Attention to detail
- Good organizational skills
- Positive attitude
- Ability to maintain total confidentiality
- Ability to prioritize and manage multiple tasks
- Excellent communication skills
- Autonomy
- Creativity
- Diplomacy
- Timeliness
- Ability to react/not overreact
- Assertiveness/self-confidence
- Familiarity working with academic departments (faculty and staff)
- Solid one-on-one relationship with department chairs, center directors, and other leadership positions
- Good understanding of the organization's operations and the inter-relationships between departments
- Extensive knowledge about the institution, local city, and surrounding areas
- Good understanding of university policies
- Dedication to the institution and community
- Technical skills (e.g., database management, Web publishing)

(Adapted from Biebuyck and Mallon, 2002)

The Dean's Charge

Once the dean, CEO, or hiring authority has appointed a search committee and its chair, that person must "charge" the committee. A crucial component of the charge is to emphasize the primacy of the search committee in the process. If the process is to have credibility, and therefore attract the most talented candidates, the dean has to clarify that no candidate will be considered whose name has not been generated through the committee nomination and evaluation process.

The dean's charge also must define:

- A **description** of the sort of department, center, or unit that the institution desires and its anticipated focus. Insofar as possible, the dean should share a summary report of the departmental review.

- The **breadth of the search**—national/international/internal search?

17

- The **screening process**—External candidates only? Will internal candidates be considered? Only internal candidates? (University policies might disallow this latter option.)

- The **responsibilities and leadership characteristics of the position** being sought.

- **Precise instructions** related to the number of finalist candidates to be identified, the composition of this group (e.g., inclusion of women and minority candidates), and the fact that the finalists should be presented in alphabetical order.

- **Guidelines** for the composition of the detailed position description and advertisements and protocols for the placement of advertisements.

- **Detailed instructions for "casting the net"**
  Casting the net includes communication about the position to deans, chairs, teaching hospital CEOs, and national leadership societies, among others. It also involves calls to selected key leaders in the field. The hiring authority will also emphasize expectations for:
  a) A proactive approach to identifying women candidates
  b) A proactive approach to identifying minority candidates
  c) Internal candidates. These candidates "raise some of the most delicate and vexing issues faced by the search committee" (McLaughlin & Riesman, 1990, p. 243).

- **Clear instructions about the confidentiality** of the entire search and screen process. Some institutions of higher education ask search committee members to sign confidentiality agreements or codes of conduct. See Appendix 2 for a template. See page 31 for a further discussion of confidentiality.

- The **education of the search committee** about identifying the essential leadership characteristics not identifiable in "traditional" academic curriculum vitae and bibliographies. Historically, some search committees evaluate candidates for leadership positions such as department chairs and center directors by counting publications and adding up grant dollars. While such tendencies pervade academe in faculty hiring, the best search committees for leadership positions should resist this habit and instead focus on the evaluation of leadership skills and potential.

- The **definition of the responsibilities** of search committee members. For example, the committee chair must inform the members precisely who will be responsible for due diligence telephone calls regarding leading candidates. (See page 42 for more information on this topic.)

- The **timetable for the search** and the date by which the dean expects to be presented with the short list.

"The best search committees for leadership positions focus on the evaluation of leadership skills and potential."

4 Candidate Attributes and Skill Sets

Identifying the required competencies, skill sets, and attributes needed for a leadership position in medical schools and teaching hospitals is not a search committee function alone. Rather, this process begins with the pre-search process of departmental and organizational reflection. Following the departmental review, as the dean or the CEO defines a vision for the future of the department or unit, she or he should produce an analysis and statement of the required knowledge, attributes, skills, and experience required by the candidate filling the position.

Past- vs. Future-Orientation*

While the traditional search process may have been an effective way to select leaders for medical schools, we question its efficacy in selecting candidates with the necessary attributes needed in today's complex environment of academic medicine. In the past, search committees understandably identified key factors such as a candidate's national prominence and personal track record in research, clinical care, and education. In addition, search committees focused on easily measured criteria, such as the candidate's publication record, history of securing extramural funding, and awards and honors. Search committees rarely considered attributes such as an understanding of the business of medicine, communication skills, ability to confront and resolve conflicts, management of faculty talent, and ability to tolerate ambiguity.

Organizational leaders and search committees need to confront the misalignment between the desires of the typical search committee and the new skills required of leadership positions such as department chairs and center directors. Is it prudent for the search committee to identify candidates by using many outdated criteria and focusing on individual achievement?

We believe that an orientation toward the future and a focus on collective achievement may be better markers of success. Even in the best circumstances, when an abundance of information about the candidate is available, it is difficult to know how a candidate will perform in a leadership position. Successfully recruiting, retaining, and sustaining "future-oriented" leaders require a different approach.

Chapter Digest

Leaders in academic medical centers should embody an orientation toward the future and a focus on collective achievement. These characteristics may include:

* Business and administrative experience
* Institutional mindset
* Emotional competence
* Resilience
* Fit with organizational values and principles
* Strong communication skills
* Ability to build and lead a team
* Results orientation
* Ability to develop others

(See pages 20–21.)

---

* This section is adapted, with permission, from Grigsby RK, Hefner DS, Souba WW, Kirch DG. The future-oriented department chair. *Acad Med.* 2004; 79: 571-577.

Innovations at Work:
Defining Leadership Expectations and Responsibilities

While the specific leadership skill sets needed in a role may vary from position to position, some attributes cut across positions. At the University of Wisconsin School of Medicine and Public Health, all department chairs receive a list of leadership responsibilities in their letters of appointment. These responsibilities include:

- Accomplishing department-related objectives of the organization's strategic plan and achieving selected performance targets established by the dean with the chair.
- Facilitating the career development of junior faculty in the department.
- Proactively supporting recruitment of female and ethnic minority. faculty to meet the school's diversity goals. Chairs are expected to assure a gender-friendly environment and salary equity for all faculty.

See the complete document in Appendix 3.

"Future-oriented leaders are self-aware and adaptive."

The Future-Oriented Leader in Academic Medicine

The characteristics and skill sets common in future-oriented leaders in academic medicine include, but are not limited to, the following:

- *Interdependent Financial Approach*
Many organizations now realize that they can no longer afford to waste time, energy, or resources on internal struggles between units. New demands require that all departments meet or exceed financial expectations, all while actively supporting their interdependence. Leaders must be facile with the operational and fiscal aspects of the unit, as well as with connections to cross-organizational initiatives such as service lines, programs, centers, and institutes.

- *Institutional Orientation*
Much has been written of the insular or "silo" approach of academic medicine in years past—this departmental hegemony led units to compete with each other for limited resources. In contrast, the future-oriented leader should think and operate from simultaneous yet disparate points of view, linking departmental and institutional priorities. Adopting an institutional perspective helps the leader to see the "big picture" and break through the insularity of the departmental structure that too often leads to internal competition for scarce resources.

- *Resilience*
Resilience, the ability to rebound from setbacks or failure, is a skill learned typically "on the job." Moving out of one's comfort zone and accepting new challenges involves risk. Leaders need to learn from their own missteps and blunders. Future-oriented leaders also must have the skill to assist others in accepting and engaging in ventures that inherently involve risk.

- *Emotional Competence*
Future-oriented leaders are self-aware and adaptive. They can place themselves in others' shoes and confront difficult situations. They are able to tolerate ambiguity. The future-oriented institutional leader sees beyond the crisis du jour and considers future consequences of actions or inaction.

- *Team Development*

Building and leading teams allows the future-oriented department chair or center director to strengthen commitment and articulate a shared vision while using the collective wisdom of the team to remove obstacles to success and to provide resources. Strong communication skills, including the ability to truly listen, are important in building trust and, ultimately, in building teams.

- *Results Orientation*

Future-oriented leaders focus on execution and subsequent outcomes. Doing so requires setting clear expectations and holding responsible parties accountable.

- *Developing Others*

Leaders should be available to mentor junior faculty while meeting the operational and financial needs of the department and institution. Learning to share leadership and to shine in the reflected light of others' performances, while aligning the faculty and staff with the institutional strategy, have become much more important in today's environment.

Helping others discover their own talents and develop new skills requires a reorientation away from the self and toward the development of others. Coaching, mentoring, and encouraging others energizes them to work toward and build a better future.

Table 4.1 shows the principal characteristics that have been sought in "traditional" department chairs and the key skills and abilities fundamental to the success of future-oriented leaders. Leaders with these abilities can craft a strategic vision to which everyone in the unit is committed and contributes. Strategic vision helps members of the department or unit deal with change and reflects good organizational health.

"Helping others discover their own talents and develop new skills requires a reorientation away from the self and toward the development of others."

Table 4.1
Characteristics of Traditional versus Future-Oriented Leaders
in Academic Medicine*

Characteristic	Example
Traditional institutional leaders (department chair, center director, etc.)	
National stature and visibility	Prominence and distinction among peers nationally
Recruitment from a prestigious institution	Comes from an academic medical center that has a solid reputation
Track record in research	Externally funded; publications in prestigious journals
Clinical competency	Recognized as a legitimate practicing physician with expertise in a particular field
Appreciation for teaching	Understands the educational and training needs of residents and medical students
"Gets along well with others"	Reasonable social skills

Characteristic	Example
Future-oriented institutional leader	
Business and administrative experience	Understands the economics and interdependence of patient care, research, and education; familiar with mission-based management
Institutional orientation	Able to balance departmental affairs with institutional priorities
Emotional competence	Self-aware and adaptive
Resilience	Does not panic after a poor financial quarter, but takes decisive action
Fit with the organization's values and guiding principles	Is a team player cognizant that her or his success is tied to the success of others
Strong communication skills	Is a good listener
Able to build and lead a team	Articulates a shared vision; removes obstacles to success, creates commitment, provides resources
Results orientation	Focuses on execution, sets clear expectations, and holds people accountable

*Adapted, with permission, from Grigsby RK, Hefner DS, Souba WW, Kirch DG. The future-oriented department chair. *Acad Med* 2004; 79: 574.

The Dean/CEO's Role:

Integrating Desired Leadership Attributes into the Search Process

An essential next step in the search process is for the dean or CEO to articulate the defining characteristics of the successful leader for the search committee prior to beginning any searching or screening. Taking the time now to draw a comprehensive "portrait" of the ideal candidate, including those elusive leadership qualities vital to success, can help eliminate valuable time spent by committee members in pursuing candidates who do not possess all the required attributes for success in the role.

The dean or CEO and the search committee chair should:
- Engage the committee in discussion of the departmental review, the dean's vision, and the department's objectives.
    o It may be important at this stage to work with an impartial facilitator, particularly if it is known or suspected that some committee members have differing views or opinions about the analysis, the future, or the process.
- Assist committee members in examining preconceived ideas or impressions of the "ideal" candidate, particularly those impressions based on past experience, former departmental activities, or a "favored" applicant. Members' strongly held preferences or biases often minimize or marginalize candidates with the very characteristics identified as most important for the goals of the department or unit.
- These characteristics then must be hard-wired into the search process itself so that the committee faithfully reviews and evaluates candidates with those attributes in mind. Chapter 7 will review techniques to ensure integration of leadership attributes into the search process.

5 Diversity and Bias in the Search Process

Unconscious Bias*

Although the number of women and minority faculty members in academic medicine and other higher education institutions has increased over time, these groups still occupy few positions of leadership within medical schools and teaching hospitals. For example, while women represented 40 percent of assistant professors in 2007-08, they comprised only 27 percent of division chiefs, 14 percent of department chairs, and 11 percent of medical school deans (AAMC, 2008). Why do academic medicine, higher education, and other professional fields still struggle with tapping the talent of women and leaders of color? While some discrimination in the recruitment process may still occur through the conscious choices and actions of those who make hiring decisions, an increasingly cited explanation is the theory of unconscious bias.

Unconscious bias refers to social stereotypes about certain demographics or groups of people that individuals form outside of their own conscious awareness. Researchers argue that most people have some degree of unconscious bias, because it stems from our natural tendency to make associations to help us organize our social worlds (Banaji, Bazerman, & Chugh, 2003). For people involved in leadership recruitment in academic medicine, an understanding of unconscious bias is important because of its potential to hinder objective evaluations of job candidates.

The Research on Unconscious Bias

Empirical research supports the existence of unconscious bias through several different methodologies. The most popular and direct way of assessing unconscious bias is through the Implicit Association Test (IAT), which has consistently demonstrated that people unconsciously prefer white over black, young over old, and thin over fat, and that people have stereotypic associations linking males with science and careers and females with liberal arts and family (Nosek, Banaji, & Greenwald, 2002).

Experimental studies also have provided evidence for unconscious biases. For example, in one study, academic psychologists evaluated the curriculum vitae of a faculty job applicant or a tenure candidate that was randomly assigned a male or female name (Steinpres, Anders, & Ritzke, 1999). Both male and female psychologists were more likely to recommend hiring the male applicant than the female applicant as a fellow faculty member, and were more likely to report that the male applicant had adequate experience in research, teaching, and service. Furthermore, the psychologists were more likely to write comments of concern in the margins of their questionnaires for the female tenure candidate than for the male tenure candidate. In a similar experiment, 155 white male participants evaluated a fictitious resume with an Asian,

Chapter Digest

To attract women and minority candidates for leadership positions in academic medicine, search committees can:

* Make the search open, not closed
* Network
* Evaluate institutional prestige in appropriate context
* Be careful of shifting filters during the evaluation of candidates as the search progresses
* Create interview environments that are welcoming and enjoyable for all
(See page 28.)

"Most people have some degree of unconscious bias, because it stems from our natural tendency to make associations to help us organize our social worlds."

---

* This section is adapted from Corrice A. "Unconscious bias in faculty and leadership recruitment: A literature review." *AAMC Analysis in Brief*, August 2009. Used with author permission.

black, Hispanic, or white name based on intelligence, motivation, and likelihood to be hired (King et al, 2006). The resume with a black name was rated least positively and the resume with an Asian name was rated most positively.

Research in real-life settings highlights the practical ramifications of unconscious bias in the hiring and evaluation process. For example, in a real-life examination of 312 letters of recommendation that helped medical school faculty receive their clinical and research positions, researchers found that, relative to male faculty, letters of recommendation for female faculty were shorter in length, were more likely to be letters of "minimal assurance" (e.g., lacking in specificity), included more gender terms (e.g., "she is an intelligent young *lady*"), and included more "doubt raisers," such as criticisms, hedges, or faint praise (Trix & Psenka, 2003). This study suggests that unconscious bias in the search and selection process for academic positions can lead evaluators to judge men's accomplishments more positively than women's.

These various types of studies supporting the existence of career-related unconscious bias against women and African Americans are summarized in Table 5.1.

"Unconscious biases are likely to affect the evaluations of and decisions made by those involved in the search and recruitment process in all settings, including academic medicine."

Implications for the Search Process

As demonstrated by the preceding examples, unconscious biases are likely to affect the evaluations of and decisions made by those involved in the search and recruitment process in all settings, including academic medicine. Because it is particularly difficult to grapple with psychological obstacles outside of conscious awareness, those involved in search and recruitment processes must be resolute to overcome unconscious bias. The following suggestions may mitigate some of the effects of unconscious bias in evaluations of job candidates.

1. Leaders of the search process can remove subjectivity from interviewing by creating more objective, structured interviews. Search committees can:
   a. Set criteria or use objective measures to assess the skills needed for effective job performance;
   b. Train search committees and others involved in the process on how to conduct structured interviews;
   c. Use performance, satisfaction, and turnover rates of new hires to measure effectiveness of the interview process (Graves, 1989).
2. Interviewers may consider that cultural differences affect first impressions of candidates. For instance, the standard American interview uses the criteria of self-confidence, goal orientation, enthusiasm, and leadership, though these qualities may not be apparent in people of more reserved cultures (Mahoney, 1992).
3. Ample time should be reserved for interviews and evaluations of candidates, as gender bias emerges more when evaluators are under time pressure (Martell, 1991).
4. Evaluators should be aware that recommenders of applicants may hold unconscious biases, and therefore may present skewed representations of applicants in their letters of recommendation (Trix & Psenka, 2003).

Table 5.1
Studies supporting the existence of career-related unconscious bias

Method	Results
Goldin & Rouse (2000)	
To test for sex-biased hiring in symphony orchestras, the researchers compared two audition procedures: "blind" auditions (adopted in 1970—involves the use of screens to conceal candidates' identities) and "not-blind" auditions (no use of screens).	• Blind auditions increases the likelihood that a female will be hired by 25%. • The switch to blind auditions in 1970 explains 30% of the increase in the proportion of females among new hires.
Heilman & Okimoto (2007)	
Given descriptions of fictitious male and female managers who were successful in male-dominated jobs, undergraduate participants evaluated the managers on several measures, including likeability, interpersonal hosility, competence, and desirability as a boss.	• Female managers were rated as more interpersonally hostile, less competent, and less desirable as bosses than were male managers.
Wennerås & Wold (1997)	
The researchers evaluated whether the peer-review system of postdoctoral fellowships at the Swedish Medical Research Council was biased against women.	• For peer-reviewers to equally rate men and women on scientific competency, women needed an equivalent of approximately three more articles in Nature or Science, or 20 more articles in a specialist journal, such as Neuroscience or Radiology.
Bertrand & Mullainathan (2003)	
To examine the effect of race on receiving job callbacks, the researchers responded with fictitious resumes to help-wanted ads in Boston and Chicago newspapers. The resumes were altered from actual ones found on job search websites. The researchers categorized the new resumes as high or low quality and assigned an equal amount black names (e.g., Lakisha) or white names (e.g., Greg).	• Resumes with white names had a 50% greater chance of receiving a callback than did resumes with black names (10.08% vs. 6.70%, respectively). • Higher quality resumes elicited 30% more callbacks for whites, whereas they only elicited 9% more callbacks for blacks. • Employers who listed "Equal Opportunity Employer" in their ad discriminated just as much as other employers.
Biernat & Manis (1994)	
143 white undergraduate participants viewed 40 photographs of black and white individuals, each paired with definitions of two words. The participants rated the verbal ability of the photographed individuals as if those individuals had provided the definitions.	• Black individuals were rated as having lower verbal ability than white individuals, suggesting that the participants had a bias that blacks are less verbally skilled than whites.

Pathways to Achieving a Diverse Leadership Team

The diversity of workforce in the nation's medical schools will continue to expand. U.S. census figures indicate that, by 2050, one of every two U.S. workers will be a person of color: African American, Hispanic, Asian American, Pacific Islander, or Native American. Given this reality, medical school leaders should attend to ways to attract minorities and women in positions of leadership.

Work by Valian (2008) suggests medical schools and teaching hospitals can:

- Make sure the search looks open rather than closed. A personal phone call from the dean to potential women and minority candidates can send the message that the school is truly interested in having a broad search. Women and members of ethnic groups may express interest differently. Don't assume that a women or minority would not consider moving to your location (because of geographic location, lack of peers or colleagues, etc.).

- Network. Attend sessions and social events at specialty or disciplinary meetings that focus on women and minorities.

- Be cautious when evaluating the prestige of a candidate's degree institution and current institution. Of all the factors that affect a faculty member's productivity, none is more powerful as institutional characteristics (Bland & Ruffin, 1992). In other words, institutional location drives productivity more than productivity determines the prestige of one's institution. A good question is whether the candidate is more productive than one might expect from an academic at this type of location?

- Set the filters that determine who moves to the next stage of consideration explicitly and appropriately. Do those filters disproportionately advantage white men? For example, will someone really make a better chair because he or she has 10 years of experience rather than 5 years? Be careful of shifting filters as the search progresses. One way to avoid this is to identify qualifications in advance.

- Create enjoyable and informative interviews with every candidate. Set up interviews for the candidates with community members about the nature of the community. Make sure the whole search committee is aware of community resources.

"A personal phone call from the dean to potential women and minority candidates can send the message that the school is truly interested in having a broad search."

6 Good Practice in Searching and Recruiting

After leaders have reviewed the department, center, or unit and defined the scope of the position in outcome terms; after the search chair has been identified and the committee formed; and after the organization's leaders and the search committee have pinpointed the essential leadership characteristics for the position, the search and recruitment process can commence.

Medical schools and teaching hospitals may vary in the mechanics of how they conduct the search. (We offer a common template that many schools generally follow.) This chapter also reviews good practice such as confidentiality, the "mechanics" of the search—such as scheduling and prospecting—and a discussion of the pros and cons of executive search firms.

Perhaps more important than these specific steps is *consistency* in the process. Consistency (in how the organization conducts one search to the next, and in how the search committee treats one candidate to the next) builds trust both internally and externally. Internally, consistency breeds confidence among faculty, administrators, staff, students, and residents that the organization is truly searching for the best possible leaders. When a search committee treats candidates consistently, the external community (both candidates and observers of the organization) can trust that the search is done with integrity and professionalism.

To be consistent, the hiring authority and search committee must ensure that every candidate comes into the search through the process as implemented by the committee. There is no place for candidates who are identified outside this process. All candidates must be considered in the same way, including internal candidates.

Chapter Digest

Good practice in the search and recruitment process:

* Consistency is key. (See below).
* When it comes to search committee size, let parsimony rule. (See page 31.)
* Institutional leaders must commit time and effort to recruit a pool of candidates. (See page 33.)
* Committees can test-run the applicant screening process to see where members agree and disagree on candidate qualifications. (See page 34.)
* Should you use a search consultant? (See pages 35–38.)

"The hiring authority and search committee must ensure that every candidate comes into the search through the process as implemented by the committee."

29

Steps for a Successful Search

While there is no single, uniform procedure, the following steps represent a common flow in many searches. A more detailed description of these steps can be found in Appendix 4.

Step 1:	Review of department	Step 18	Correspond with nominees who submit CV
Step 2:	Alignment or realignment with organizational strategy	Step 19	Plan calls to leading candidates
Step 3:	Define major qualities to be sought	Step 20	Determine candidates to be invited for visits
Step 4:	Initiate search process	Step 21	Set up first visit to the campus
Step 5:	Select chair of search committee	Step 22	Develop a list of interview questions (including behavioral questions)
Step 6:	Attend to administrative infrastructure	Step 23	Decide on the interview panel and arrange the schedule
Step 7:	Decide whether to hire search consultant	Step 24	Offer training to committee and interviewers on interviewing techniques and unconscious bias
Step 8:	Appoint search committee membership	Step 25	Interviewers meet candidates and write evaluations
Step 9:	Announce the search	Step 26	Identify small number (2-5) of semi-finalists; learn about personal needs and interests
Step 10:	Set date for first meeting	Step 27	Attend to the subtleties of the interview schedule
Step 11:	Determine agenda for first meeting	Step 28	Hold seminars and social interactions
Step 12	Arrange advertisements	Step 29	Determine list of finalists
Step 13	Write letters requesting nominations	Step 30	Search chair makes reference calls
Step 14	Make calls to establish network	Step 31	Committee presents dean or CEO with unranked list of 2 or more finalists
Step 15	Establish log	Step 32	Hiring authority contacts additional references; conducts reverse site visits
Step 16	Acknowledge submitted nominations and applications	Step 33	Hiring authority makes selection
Step 17	Develop candidate evaluation form	Step 34	Write close-off letters

A Note from the Dean….

Communicating about the Search

The launch of the search is a critical time for the dean or CEO to communicate to the whole community about the process. The organizational leader should provide information about the findings of the pre-search work, including an indication to the community about the future direction of the department or unit. Such clarity will go a long way toward alleviating the stress associated with a change in leadership and direction.

Communication should
- Effectively signal the importance of the position to the organization
- Encourage members of the community to broadcast the opening
- Allow for recommendations of potential candidates to the committee
- Help the committee, the dean's office, and the department or unit in championing whatever organizational change may be required as the new position is filled

Confidentiality and Disclosure in Searches

Leaders in academic medical centers face two forces during the search process: the need for confidentiality and the desire for transparency. Often, people treat these forces as oppositional. We do not believe confidentiality and transparency are antonyms.

Search experts agree that confidentiality is essential in successful searches for leadership positions (Hochel & Wilson, 2007; Marchese & Lawrence, 2006; McLaughlin, 1985). Organizational pressures for information about the status of the search can quickly manifest, and the search committee must be prepared with clear expectations and guidelines.

Steps to Ensure Confidentiality
1. Let parsimony rule: keep the search committee size small. Experts suggest that 10 or fewer members is optimal; 5-7 members may be ideal (Marchese & Lawrence, 2006; Sessa & Taylor, 2000; Vicker & Royer, 2005). Not only is confidentiality easier to maintain with a smaller committee size, but scheduling is easier, too.
2. During the dean's charge at the very first search committee meeting, the dean should empower *only* the chair to speak for the committee at any stage. Calls to candidates, or references during the "due diligence" and selection process, should be made only by the hiring authority, the chair, or someone who is specifically designated with those tasks.
3. The search chair should constantly reinforce the message about the importance of confidentiality. Confidentiality can be breached anywhere, not just in the committee.
4. Ask committee members to sign a code of conduct, which includes a statement about confidentiality. See Appendix 2 for a template of a code of conduct.

5. Hold the committee accountable. If a committee member breaches confidentiality egregiously, that individual should be removed from the committee. The chair should discuss the breach directly with the whole committee.

6. Remind those involved in the search that confidentiality continues after the search, too. It is permanent.

7. Have a game plan ready if confidentiality is breached. For example, who will call the candidate about the breach?

8. Remind the search committee that the most serious breaches of confidentiality are quite often the result of off-hand (or even "off the record") conversations with colleagues. A candidate whose current position is jeopardized or lost as a direct result of a third-party disclosure about his or her candidacy for another position may file suit for wrongful discharge against the institution and any of its involved leaders or representatives.

The relationships among search committee members play an important role in the entire conduct of the search process, including maintaining confidentiality. From the outset, the search chair should promote a friendly and respectful attitude among committee members. Often, this takes several meetings and social occasions to achieve. Once again, this process underlines the importance of selecting members interested in furthering the missions and goals of the entire institution and not just the interests of their own constituencies or their personal interests.

What Not to Do: Examples of Breaches of Confidentiality

We have gathered the following examples from academic medical centers across the country of searches going off-track when confidentiality was lost:

- A committee member took it upon himself to call the candidate's colleagues before the candidate was ready to disclose that she was being considered for the position. When she became aware of this, she withdrew.

- One institution had an internal candidate as well as several external candidates. One of the search committee members worked in the same department as the internal candidate and shared what was being said at the search committee meetings with the internal candidate.

- The search committee received the CVs and interview reports of the candidates one week prior to the meeting of the committee. At the meeting, one of the committee members said, "I called my friend who works at the same institution as the candidate to check him out, and I found out he's pretty good, so I think we should meet him."

- Through a slip of the tongue, an interviewer told one candidate the name of another candidate who interviewed recently.

- The incumbent department chair, who was kept in the loop as the search progressed but was not a member of the search committee, disclosed to the members of the department the names of the candidates who were being considered before any of them were ready to disclose that fact to their home institutions. This resulted in people outside of the search committee and the department knowing who was being considered for the position. Later on during the search, a member of another department revealed to a colleague of one of the candidates that she was being considered for this position. Upon learning of this disclosure, the candidate withdrew.

The Mechanics of the Search and Recruitment Process

Scheduling
A typical complaint about the search process is that it takes too long. According to a 2009 AAMC survey, the average length of the search process for medical school department chairs was 12 months. The process can be an emotional rollercoaster for candidates and for interim leaders.

If the process drags too long, the candidates become fatigued and, at times, withdraw their candidacy. For those searches involving very specific skill and experience requirements, time may mean another institution with more streamlined processes and tighter scheduling is able to lure the perfect candidate while your administrator works to get a quorum together.

One reason that the process gets drawn out is scheduling. At the first search committee meeting, committee members should put on their calendars all subsequent meetings and interview dates, up and through the finalist interviews. A general rule of thumb is two days of interviewing time for semi-finalists and, two weeks later, another two days of interviewing time for finalists.

Prospecting and Recruiting
In the days of yore, some search committees had the tendency to place advertisements in prominent journals and then… wait. Today, few institutions have that luxury—and probably fewer than the number that think they do. Medical schools and teaching hospitals need to let the market know about the search. According to Hoffmeir (2003):

> Unless your institution is renowned and/or the organization's clinical or research specialty for which you plan to conduct the chair search is renowned, candidates won't be pounding at your door for the job. As painful as it may be to acknowledge, unless you are a market leader, the success of your search will depend on your ability to uncover the prized candidate—he or she won't simply appear on your doorstep one day….

> …With the exception of superstar institutions or departments, you must sell your position. A question that the search committee must take the time to answer honestly at the onset is this: Why would someone be interested in this position? If that question can't be answered, the search is going to go nowhere fast. Another point—throwing money at your dream candidate will rarely work. Certainly, money talks, but its allure will rarely be so great that other critical factors about the organization, the department, or the job will be overlooked. (pp. 125, 126)

Unfortunately, most search committees stop short of doing the deep networking and prospecting that they need to. How many leads you need depends on who you ask. Search consultants advise that a good search means a database of 200-300 names—based on the idea that searches are probability exercises: the greater the number of potential candidates, the greater likelihood of having a good outcome. For some positions and some institutions, that number may be both unrealistic and unnecessary.

Search consultants can help generate potential candidates because they are, by definition, professional networkers. For institutions that do not hire search firms,

"Most search committees stop short of doing the deep networking and prospecting that they need to."

33

the responsibility to personally tap networks and make phone calls cannot rest solely (or even primarily) with the search committee—it is an institutional responsibility. Some medical schools and teaching hospitals use "in-house" search consultants to generate leads. However, institutional leaders also have a role to play:

> A search committee, no matter how talented, seldom has the background, time, or wit for heavy-duty recruiting, which is why, more and more, search consultants are on the scene. Because of that weakness and without a search firm, institutional leaders *must* commit personal time and office resources to the recruitment function, with first responsibility being that of the appointing officer. The committee and its chair should play every apt role in recruitment, but it is the institution itself that must see to the strength of the pool. (Marchese & Lawrence, 2006, p. 38)

Screening

Chapter 7 is devoted to evaluating applicants. Here, we discuss a few important practices that committees may wish to consider:

- Spend a committee meeting on a **test-run of applicant screening**. Have all committee members evaluate the same group of applicants (3-4) and see where members agree and disagree on qualifications. Determine whether committee members interpret the desired competencies and skill sets in the same way.

  Oftentimes there can be a mismatch between the desired attributes for the position and the skills of the candidates whom the search committees choose to interview. As mentioned in chapter 4, candidates may be chosen for the weight of their CV, or the fact that they are well known to or favored by one or more members of the search committee, rather than for their leadership qualities. Good candidates with excellent management skills may be inadvertently screened out because their academic CV doesn't compare to "academic powerhouses" with hefty CVs. Academic medicine can also display a "rock star" culture, and the committee can be too pedigree-driven. A mock screening exercise can identify and rectify the gaps between what the institution desires and what the committee may desire, however unrealistic.

- Marchese and Lawrence (2006) recommend that committee members "watch your mindset" and **avoid looking for excuses to eliminate candidates**. "It's at this point that mistakes are made, that the nontraditional or unusual candidacy is lost, that the pool gets stripped down to a midlevel common denominator. That mindset also may be why some women or minority candidates get lost" (p. 53).

- Consider the candidates' points of view and **keep them informed along the way**. The search and selection process is full of anxiety for candidates who are considering the position. Inform them about the stages of the search process and where they stand. Send timely, courteous, and respectful letters to those candidates whom you have eliminated from consideration. Search consultants may agree to personally deliver this news to candidates. However, a formal letter from the organization should follow.

- **Avoid pursuing one candidate too early in the process.** The pitfall of "early" courting is that if the recruitment of one candidate is unsuccessful, the search process must begin over—amounting to a large waste of time. Moreover, premature candidate selection indicates a less-than-rigorous process; other promising candidates may bow out. Premature selection can undermine the entire search process—for the committee, for the department or unit, and for the institution.

Sometimes, search committees are simply responding to dire-sounding needs of top prospects who try to impose early deadlines. Proceed with caution! These candidates may not really be interested in your position—rather, they may want to use your offer as a bargaining chip with another recruitment offer. The best way to proceed if candidates press for an immediate decision is to explain your own timetable and request their understanding. If they are truly committed to your position, typically they will stay with the process. Remember, too, even if you are informed of an offer from a competing institution, it is unwise and a serious breach of confidentiality and privacy to contact the competitor for information or to in any manner attempt to interfere in its dealings with the candidate.

Search Consultants

The use of search consultants in academe started with positions that most resembled the private sector and had the most competition from outside the academy—namely deans of business schools and medical schools (Stein & Trachtenberg, 1993). Institutions hire search consultants in hopes of finding candidates otherwise missed by the usual "net." Search consultants can educate committee members about the importance of confidentiality and the damage of breaches or leaks on both the search and the careers of candidates.

A search consultant is not necessary to conduct an effective search if institutional leaders have the energy, patience, resources, and, most importantly, time. However, search consultants can help the search committee chair cope with the additional pressures of the search commitments in additional to his or her regular job.

Even today, with search firms more common in leadership-level recruitment, many in academic medicine remain skeptical of the use of any consultants. Faculty may resist the idea of "headhunters." Some may view the use of a search firm as a sign of failure—that the school cannot successfully recruit a leader on its own. At the same time, *not* using a search firm might indicate to some that the position is not important to the institution.

A challenge to using search firms is to ensure that they *consult* with the search committee but do not *control* the search. Professional search consultants are very careful not to preempt the function and work of the search committee, but rather try to work in partnership and defer to the committee chair in the presence of other committee members.

Bennis and O'Toole (2000) emphasize that institutional leaders and boards should "keep control of the search" (p. 173). They point out that search firms follow the guidance of their clients—a reasonable strategy provided that the guidance is sound. Search firms should be the "arms and legs" of the search and serve as an independent sounding board, but should never be the decision maker.

"A challenge to using search firms is to ensure that they consult with the search committee but do not control the search."

Organizational leaders and search committees need to be aware of potential bias of the search consultant toward particular types of candidates. Firms may be risk-adverse—advocating for the usual suspects rather than innovative, bold, and perhaps riskier candidates. Since most executive search firms "guarantee" their work (for example, re-doing the search if the leader stays less than a year in the position), there may be a financial incentive to recommend less innovative candidates as a means for ensuring success.

The AAMC's Leadership Search Advisory Committee, comprised of medical school and teaching hospital faculty and administrators who run search processes for their institutions, offered the following advice to ensure successful engagements with search firms:

1. Request transparency in how the firm creates their list of candidates. Firms that simply tap an existing database or make inquiries to particular groups of institutions may inject a skewed roster of candidates, without the search committee's awareness. Know how the candidate list was generated, not just who is on it.
2. Set clear expectations about responsibilities and deliverables. In the contract, identify detailed deliverables at each step of the way.
3. Be clear about who is doing the work. The principal or other staff? Or the client?
4. Ask for a clear statement of what efforts they take to help create a diverse pool of candidates. Are they aware of the research on unconscious bias? What is their track record on placing women and minorities into leadership positions?
5. Do reference checking on the firm and the specific consultant with whom you will work.

See Appendix 5 for suggestions and questions when engaging an executive search firm.

The Cost and Benefit of Search Firms
The cost of hiring search consultants varies but often approximates one-third of first-year compensation for the new leadership position, plus expenses of consultant travel, lodging, and other incidentals during the search. These arrangements may create the appearance of a conflict of interest (if not a real conflict) as the search firm has a financial incentive to drive the first-year salary as high as possible—a higher salary brings higher consulting fees.

There are exceptions to this standard. For example, some firms charge a fixed fee amount. We are aware of at least one medical school that purchased a "package" of searches from one firm because administrators knew they would do a number of searches over a period of 2-3 years. The per-search cost when purchased in bulk was far less expensive than would have been the case if purchased separately. (The risk of this approach is that search firm might be complacent when they know that they have secured multiple engagements up front—and if the school is dissatisfied with the firm's performance, they don't have the option of hiring a different firm.)

Increasingly, institutional leaders view the use of search consultants positively because they recognize that hiring mistakes can be extremely expensive. As McLaughlin (1993) noted, consultant fees are quite small compared with the "expense of launching another search or suffering through the trauma of a poor selection" (p. 155). The cost of hiring a search consultant may be less expensive than the institutional cost of a failed search, especially if one includes "lost opportunity" costs

"Increasingly, institutional leaders view the use of search consultants positively because they recognize that hiring mistakes can be extremely expensive."

expended by the members of the search committee (and particularly by the committee chair).

In a 2009 survey of medical school deans, the use of search firms was far more common for clinical department chairs than other leadership positions: search firms were retained for 26 percent of clinical department chair searches, but only for 4 percent of basic science chair searches and 6 percent of major center director searches (Mallon & Corrice, 2009). We anticipate that medical schools and teaching hospitals will continue to collaborate with professional search firms for two reasons. First, three of four deans reported being satisfied with their experiences with search firms—a good indicator of repeat business. Second, search committee members often do not have adequate time to commit to the rigors of the search process. Committee members who don't have professional assistance are becoming increasingly stressed by the effort required to complete the task.

The Pros and Cons of Using Search Consultants

Pros

- Brings credibility to the search process. Using a search process signals to both internal and external communities that the position is of critical importance to the organization, and that it will be an open and professional process.
- Usually develops a more comprehensive position statement/job description (sometimes called the "scoping document") than institutional experts.
- Can help the search committee chair cope with the additional pressures of the search requirements in addition to his or her regular responsibilities.
- Gain valuable insights by interviewing cross-section of institutional leaders about the characteristics to be sought in candidates.
- Serve as an invaluable "neutral party" in the assessment of internal candidates and their comparison to outside candidates.
- Can signal to external candidates that the search is truly national in scope and not a façade in favor of an internal candidate.
- Can gently "let down" internal candidates when necessary, saving emotional confrontation and/or diffusing anger.
- Can be of great assistance to the search committee in analyzing in depth the "dazzling resume" of candidates skilled in the art of self-promotion. Search consultants can spend hours with such a candidate, and give a detailed report to the committee (McLaughlin & Riesman, 1990, p. 245).
- Keep in touch with candidates about the progress of the search, and make up for the abysmal behavior of some search committees in "leaving candidates wondering if they have been dropped from consideration" (McLaughlin & Riesman, 1990, p. 248).
- Help the committee maintain confidentiality.
- Can shorten the length of the search (25% shorter, on average, for clinical department chair searches, based on 2009 AAMC survey data). By bringing professional expertise, the firm can keep the search committee on track, aid in scheduling and screening, and close the search faster.

The Pros and Cons of Using Search Consultants (cont.)

Pros (cont.)

- Can be effective in negotiations.
- Can persuade reluctant candidates, who refuse to respond to the usual letters of inquiry and nomination, to consider the position.
- Can maintain more detailed records and manage data required for affirmative action, equal employment opportunity, or organizational diversity compliance.

Cons

- Search consultants are costly.
- A consultant may simply not understand academe in general and academic medicine in particular.
- A consultant who does not spend enough time interviewing a wide cross-section of the campus may see the institution only through the eyes of its leaders.
- Some candidates do not respond well to overtures from consultants.
- Consultants may be biased in presenting the strongest case to the search committee for the candidates they know well and favor.
- If the consultant does most of the work, committee members may not feel involved in the process or in the finalists. They may "refuse to accept the search consultant's recommended candidates, or worse, they may lack a feeling of investment in the final candidate" (Touchton, 1989, p. 9).
- Consultants may have potential conflict of interest, recommending candidates simultaneously to different searches.
- Candidates may get different messages from a search committee chair and consultant.
- The consultant may be "over-extended" and delegate tasks to her or his staff despite originally promising to be personally involved at all times.
- The search committee has no way of knowing "whether the finalists identified by the consultant are typical representatives of a larger cohort or represent just about all the available possibilities" (McLaughlin & Riesman, 1990, p. 258).

7 Evaluating Candidates

As noted in Chapter 4, the dean, hospital director, or hiring authority must articulate the leadership competencies and attributes needed for the position. But these characteristics then must be hard-wired into the search process itself so that the committee will faithfully review and evaluate candidates with those attributes in mind.

Medical schools and teaching hospitals can ensure this integration through a variety of methods, including CV and interview evaluation tools, interview question lists, and candidate statements. Below, we include many ideas, tools, and methods for evaluating candidates for the essential qualities required in department chairs, center directors, and other important leadership positions.

Candidate "Statements"

Some academic medical centers ask for more than just a CV, which, by nature, summarizes past accomplishments and outputs. These organizations also request a statement from each candidate about their leadership philosophy (e.g., in research, education, clinical care, administration, management, mentoring, etc.). These statements provide insight into the candidate's vision, philosophy, values, and approach—which then can be evaluated in relation to the desired attributes for the position.

These statements may take the form of a cover letter. The level of detail that the candidate expresses about the organization in the cover letter may be a good indicator of both the candidate's authentic interest in the position and his or her initiative.

The Cover Letter

A candidate's cover letter is her or his opportunity to fill in the gaps of a CV (Will, 2009). Does the candidate come from a nontraditional career path or is there an unusual career trajectory? Search committees should pay attention to the cover letter for explanation and insight.

Much can be learned and inferred from a cover letter (Will, 2009):

- **Is it well written?** Typos and misspellings demonstrate carelessness.
- **Is it brief?** Cover letters that go on for pages and pages can indicate an inability to be clear and succinct or a grandiose sense of self.
- **Does it read like a form letter?** The candidate should have taken the time to tailor her or his letter to your institution and your position. Do candidates explain why they are interested in this specific position?
- **Does the cover letter address the needs and aspirations of your organization?** A cover letter should talk about the candidate's qualifications and skill sets, to be sure. But it also should explain how those qualifications match with your organization's needs. Candidates' cover letters should demonstrate that they have done their homework about the position and the organization.
- **Does it address gaps or questions in one's CV?** The candidate should anticipate what questions the committee might have about qualifications or career path and address those questions in the cover letter.

Chapter Digest

Among the tools available to evaluate candidates, search committees can use:

* Candidate statements (see below).
* Behavioral interviewing (see page 40).
* Leadership competency evaluation forms (see page 41).
* Formal assessment tools (see page 41).
* Reverse site visits (see page 43).
* 360-degree reference checking (see page 42).
* Reverse reference-checking (see page 43).

"The leadership competencies and attributes needed for the position must be hard-wired into the search process itself."

Behavioral Interviewing

Candidates should be interviewed with the desired leadership attributes in mind. Many search committees develop a set of interview questions that they ask of every candidate. Behavioral interviewing is increasingly common as a technique to understand candidates' potential based upon actual past behaviors rather than on responses to hypothetical questions.

"Behavioral interviewing is increasingly common as a technique to understand candidates' potential based upon actual past behaviors."

In behavior-based interviews, interviewers ask the candidate about specific examples of when and how they demonstrated particular behaviors or skills. Candidates should describe a particular event, project, or experience in detail, including how they dealt with the situation and what the outcome was. See, for example, the master list of behavioral questions developed by Lehigh Valley Health Network, from which search committees draw for specific interviews (Appendix 6).

While it can be illuminating, behavioral interviewing also can have downsides. As it becomes more commonplace, candidates may be well-prepared for the technique. Questions that begin, "Tell me about a time when you…" can telegraph the desired competency—savvy candidates may "ace the interview" while having less authentic ability in the desired area. Interviewers will need to dig deeper; asking "how?" and "why?" questions can help.

Behavioral interviewing also demands that interviewees describe personal contributions instead of team outcomes. Yet people from certain ethnic traditions (and some women more than men) might be uncomfortable promoting personal contributions, preferring to emphasize group accomplishments.

Human resources experts believe that competencies and attributes that emerge naturally during the course of an interview may be more reliable and powerful than those highlighted in response to a specific question (Kennedy, 2001). Evidence of behavior that is repeated over the course of many interviews and many examples will trump a single answer.

Interviewers need to become accustomed to behavioral interviewing. A brief training session before interviews begin can be a good introduction to the behavioral interviewing process and techniques. If candidates do not describe a real situation, do not provide enough detail, or do not describe the outcome, interviewers may have to probe for more information. Sometimes behavioral interviewing can produce a period of silence as candidates think about their responses; interviewers should be coached or trained to be comfortable with those pauses and not to "rescue the candidate."

What Not to Ask During an Interview

In addition to becoming familiar with behavioral interview questions, search committees also must know what questions *not* to ask. Your organization's human resources department can provide specific guidance based on your state laws. For general principles and guidelines, see Appendix 7 on compliance with equal employment opportunity regulations and anti-discriminatory practices in interviewing.

Evaluation Forms

Many organizations develop specific feedback forms that link the desired leadership competencies to the evaluation process. Some academic medical centers use CV or interview evaluation forms to ensure that reviewers focus on important attributes. See, for example:

- Lehigh Valley Health Network developed a list of desired leadership competencies against which they evaluate candidates and current leaders. See Appendix 8.
- CV evaluation tool from Northeastern Ohio Universities College of Medicine in Appendix 9.
- Interview evaluation form from the University of Arizona College of Medicine in Appendix 10.
- Interview evaluation tool from Northeastern Ohio Universities College of Medicine in Appendix 11.

Formal Assessment Tools

In the AAMC's *Successful Medical School Department Chair*, Biebuyck and Mallon (2002) proposed that medical schools could benefit from formal assessment instruments to measure candidates' intellectual and psychological capacities and approaches to leadership and management.

While empirical data are not available, anecdotal evidence suggests that this approach has not been widely adopted by academic medicine, although it may be more common in other industries (and even then, its use is not widespread. According to Sessa and Taylor [2000], fewer than four in 10 corporate executives used assessment instruments).

Yet such assessment could be valuable to deans, hospital directors, and search committee chairs in assessing the finalists for leadership positions. Many assessment tools are available—many executive search firms have proprietary tools that they tout. Training and development companies also offer assessments. These tools tend to evaluate candidates in areas such as cognitive abilities, interpersonal communication skills, leadership styles and competencies, problem-solving skills, and work "personality." Overall, these assessments provide insight to how people approach their work.

Candidates may be understandably leery of formal assessments, if for no other reason that they are not commonly used in academic institutions. Organizations that use these tools typically do so only with finalists, and it is critical that they use them properly—that is, to analyze "fit" between organization and candidate, and not as a screening tool to "de-select" candidates. At most organizations, the candidate assessment is shared only with the search committee chair and the hiring authority—not shared with the candidate.

Reverse Site Visits

A small number of medical schools employ "reverse site visits," the technique of visiting the leading candidates at their home base and interviewing their colleagues. According to a 2009 AAMC survey, deans employed this technique in 14 percent of basic science department chair searches and in 8 percent of clinical chair searches (Mallon & Corrice, 2009).

"Many organizations develop specific feedback forms that link the desired leadership competencies to the evaluation process."

The power of reverse site visits is that they offer an important intuitive feel of the candidate on their home turf. One dean described the reverse site visit as a "Gestalt thing—you get a feel for what candidates are like just by walking into their offices." These visits provide additional perspective of how the candidates are perceived in their own environment—a broader picture of who they are.

Of course, these visits may need to be handled discreetly. Who the search committee chair, dean, or hospital director meets with during a reverse site visit will depend on the degree of sensitivity for the candidate. Some deans report meeting openly with the candidate's peers, direct reports, and current dean. In one case, a dean reported meeting off-campus in the candidate's home town.

A downside of reverse site visits is that they are time-consuming—perhaps an explanation of why they are not more common. That said, however, the time needed for a small number of visits is minimal compared to the recovery period of a failed search or a failed leader.

360-Degree Reference Checking

Most search processes include due diligence consultation—interviewing people who know the candidate in a professional setting, such as leaders in the finalists' discipline, institutional leaders, and coworkers.

"Random calls made by various search committee members to their acquaintances at the candidate's institution can be destructive."

Adapted from Bennis and O'Toole (2000), the following questions may be useful to ask the candidate's superiors, peers, and direct reports:
- Can you provide an example of how the candidate inspired followers to trust him or her?
- In what ways does the candidate energize others? Can you provide an example?
- Can you tell me how you have witnessed the candidate developing others?
- In what ways does the candidate demonstrate respect for followers? Have you witnessed situations where he or she did not?
- In what ways does the candidate demonstrate that he or she listens?
- How the candidate holds people responsible for their performance and promises?
- Have you seen the candidate delegating important tasks to others? How so?

Reference checking may be done by the hiring authority or by the search committee chair—whoever is responsible, it is preferable for the same person to make all calls so that each reviewer is asked the same questions. Random calls made by various search committee members to their "acquaintances" at the candidate's institution can be destructive, are unfair to other candidates, can undercut the candidacy of certain individuals, and should not be allowed.

While due diligence calls should be made to those references that the candidate has provided, the dean or search committee chair should not stop there. They should go "off list" to peers, collaborators, colleagues, and, most importantly, workers who report to the candidate, such as administrative assistants, nurses, students, and residents. Selected national leaders and leaders in the candidate's own institution may also be called. According to a 2009 survey, medical school deans personally called references provided by the finalists in 76 percent of department chair and center director searches and called references "off-list" in 65 percent of searches (Mallon & Corrice, 2009).

While some deans may simply inform the candidate that she or he will go off-list, others may ask the candidate if it is okay to do so. The answer to that question in and of itself may be telling. If the candidate says no, what might that reveal about the candidate?

Reverse Reference Checking

With the scrutiny that the institution gives to candidates, it is important to remember that the search process is also a *recruitment* process. So in the midst of reverse site visits, formal assessments, and reference checking of the candidate, it is equally important to give finalist candidates the ability to determine if the organization will meet his or her professional and personal goals and aspirations. One tool to provide candidates such information is through "reverse reference checking," in which the dean, hospital director, or hiring authority gives finalists a list of people with whom he or she has worked in previous positions to allow for candidates to do their own due diligence on the CEO's or dean's leadership and management style.

"It is important to give finalist candidates the ability to determine if the organization will meet his or her professional and personal goals and aspirations."

8 "Concierge-level" Service

Chapter Digest

Search committees are on the front lines of recruiting candidates. Providing "concierge-level" service to all candidates sends an important message that the institution is serious about attracting top-quality talent and is a great place to work.

Search committees can:

* Acknowledge applications promptly (see below).
* Provide detailed "dossiers" to candidates (see page 46).
* Coordinate campus visits through a recruitment coordinator (see page 46).
* Create a candidate visit "experience" (see page 46).

The "search committee" is a misnomer. In addition to having the responsibility to develop a broad candidate pool and to identify finalists for the position, these committees are on the front lines of recruiting candidates to the organization. We should refer to these groups as search and recruitment committees to keep the recruitment function top of mind.

Unfortunately, many search committee members do not commit sufficient effort to attracting top-notch candidates. The academic culture reinforces behaviors that might undermine the committee's focus on recruitment. For example, physicians and scientists in academe typically are socialized to find points of weakness in another's position, point of view, or research, and are rewarded for quick judgments. Committee members, therefore, may seem to play "gotcha" with candidates and to appear to be critical or adversarial rather than welcoming and open. This is not to say that search committee members should avoid asking tough, probing questions—rather, they need to do so in a manner that also honors their role to attract the best qualified candidates.

Search committees, and chairs in particular, also may not be attuned to the important messages conveyed by how well or poorly the logistics of candidate visits are handled:

* Does someone meet the candidate at the airport?
* Do they structure time during a visit to address the "complete" candidate—such as personal interests and hobbies, schools, real estate, and spousal/family needs? Does the committee even *know* what the candidates' personal interests and hobbies are?
* Does the interview schedule allow for a few moments of personal time during the day?

Comments from candidates who have taken the time to review this process often say that their serious consideration of the position was negatively impacted by the committee's—and thus, the institution's—attention to these critical personal details.

For schools that use search support staff professionals, attention to detail and to the logistics of campus visits convey that the organization is sincere in its interest in candidates. On the other hand, we know of one medical school that was so inattentive to the campus visit that no one from the institution attended the dinner that was arranged for the candidate because they all thought someone else was going!

Academic medical centers in general, and search committees in particular, need to see themselves as recruiters. Providing "concierge-level" service to all candidates sends an important message that the institution is serious about attracting top-quality talent and is a great place to work.

The Application Stage

While concierge-level service is especially important for the pool of finalists, a professional approach to the search and recruitment function begins with applicants

"Many search committee members do not commit sufficient effort to attracting top-notch candidates."

and those who may become applicants. Inquiries and applications must be treated confidentially and acknowledged promptly. Candidates who will not be considered further should be notified as soon as possible, with a courteous expression of appreciation for their interest. One dean personally called every woman applicant for a chair position, even those not on the short list, and thanked them for their interest.

"Search committees should aim to treat everyone in the applicant pool with dignity and respect."

Small acts go a long way in creating goodwill and improving the institution's reputation as a great place to work. Search committees should aim to treat everyone in the applicant pool with dignity and respect.

Detailed Institutional "Dossiers"

Visits to campus tend to be tightly scheduled, which leave candidates little time to obtain important perspectives and information. Sometimes candidates are left asking questions that could have been better answered in advance. Academic medical centers do themselves and candidates a huge service by providing clear and comprehensive information as preparatory materials for the visit. These institutional and departmental "dossiers" may include:

- Institutional and department strategic plans
- Institutional and departmental financials
- Institutional and departmental histories and fact sheets
- Institutional and department summaries in education, research, and clinical care
- Selected summaries or excerpts of departmental reviews
- Details on important strategic initiatives, new programs, etc.
- Brief biosketches (highly relevant information only) on all individuals with whom the candidate will meet
- Brief biosketches of other key institutional or departmental leaders
- Details of the local community and region
- Other important nonconfidential information

Candidate Visits

One goal of the candidate visit is to create an "experience" designed to enlist and engage the candidates' interest. Another principal goal of such an experience should be to ensure that each candidate goes back into the world saying good things about the process and the institution as a whole. During the candidate visit, organizations should aim for a seamless visit, with candidates cared for the entire time by one person. Such an approach ensures a friendly face—someone who is recognizable, dependable, and can act as a portal for information.

This staff "concierge" also is an important observer of candidate behavior—he or she can be witness to how the candidate interacts with and treats people at all levels in the organization—including administrative assistants, hospital staff, students, residents, and so on. These observations can be of critical importance—especially if the candidate is rude, gruff, or disrespectful when "off camera."

Innovations at Work

The Recruitment Coordinator

Ohio State University Medical Center employs a recent college graduate as a "recruitment coordinator." This individual handles senior-level recruitments in both the medical center and the medical school. Among the duties of this position are to coordinate the campus visit, secure hotel and travel accommodations, prepare a separate itinerary for a spouse or partner, and personally accompanying the candidate from arrival to departure. The goal is to develop a relationship with each candidate. The recruitment coordinator also provides important feedback to the senior vice president about each candidate based on his or her interactions with others during the visit outside of formal interviews. This view into candidate behavior can add a critical viewpoint into a candidate's potential fit with the organization's values and culture.

Finalist visits are an important time to put the institution's best, most hospitable foot forward. Typically, candidates are invited to bring their spouse or partner. The search committee or search ambassador should elicit information in advance from the candidates and partners about interests and needs and "take them where they want to go." Tapping community resources is critical, and cannot be effectively done in a day's notice. Your organization's human resources office may have "orientation packets" already prepared for staff; having the search coordinator adapt this information for leadership candidates will create a positive impression early in the "recruitment" process. Does the organization have contacts with local ethnic and racial communities, with gay/lesbian/biracial/transgendered (GLBT) groups, with faith communities, and with special needs/special education advocates and communities? Is everyone on the search committee familiar with these resources, should they be asked?

Balancing the Interview Schedule
In constructing the candidate's interview schedule, the search chair, committee, and search coordinator need to balance the interests of the candidate with the need for a standard set of interviews. It is appropriate to have a consistent—even prototypical—interview schedule so that key individuals meet all candidates for the position. However, some consideration should also be given to tailoring the interview schedule so that each candidate's interests—professional or personal—are accommodated. Like many aspects of the search process, this can be a fine balance.

"Finalist visits are an important time to put the institution's best, most hospitable foot forward."

Innovations at Work

Standardizing the Candidate Visit
Stanford University School of Medicine has developed a clear template for candidate visits for leadership-level searches.

- Arrive evening, two full days of interviews, depart late on second day
- Respond to specific questions about the "Recruitment Information Materials"
- Meetings with individuals identified by search committee and department chair
- Intended to have great breadth but not as much depth, with the idea that follow-up conversations can occur later
- Well-oiled, professional service
- Personal escort from one office to the next
- Accommodate individual requests for meetings
- Respond to additional impromptu requests
- Conduct exit interview

Day 0

Arrive evening

Day 1

7-8 am	**Breakfast with search committee chair**
8 am-12 noon	**30-40 minute meetings**
	• Key members of department (e.g., division chiefs, senior leadership)
	• Select small groups of senior and junior faculty members
	• Members of search committee
	• Hospital administration, school administration
	• Individuals of the candidate's choosing
12-1 pm	**Lunch with residents**
1-3 pm	**30-40 minute meetings**
	• Continuation of those identified above
3-4 pm	**Tour of department space**
6:30 pm	**Dinner with search committee**

Day 2

8 am-12 noon	**30-40 minute meetings**
	• Key members of department (e.g., division chiefs, senior leadership)
	• Select senior and junior faculty members
	• Members of search committee
	• Hospital administration, school administration
	• Individuals of the candidates choosing
12 noon	**Lunch with fellows**
1-3 pm	**30-40 minute meetings**
	• Continuation of above
3-4 pm	**Meet with dean**
4-5 pm	**Meet with search committee**
5 pm	**Candidate departs**
5 pm	**Executive session of search committee**

9 Recruitment of the Top Candidate

After the search committee has given their (unranked) list of finalists to the dean, CEO, or hiring authority, the responsibility for the process shifts away from the committee. After interviewing finalists, conducting reference checks, and possibly visiting candidates at their home institutions, the leader will identify the most qualified candidate.

In the case of the clinical department chair, the responsibility for negotiations and recruitment is often shared by the dean and the teaching hospital CEO. While the chair of the search committee and the members of the search committee play crucial "partnering" roles in recruitment, as do the various people in the organization who meet the candidate during the formal visits, the dean and hospital CEO now play the key role in the final recruitment and development of the recruitment package.

If medical schools and teaching hospitals are ambitious and try to attract the most outstanding candidate for each given position, they must be prepared to fail—"at least one out of five [first-choice candidates] will be likely to turn down your offer" according to experts at Harvard Business School (Fernández-Aráoz, Groysberg, & Nohria, 2009).

Several factors can influence the likelihood of a top candidate accepting an offer.

Mutual commitments

It's not only about the money. Typically, negotiations between institutional leaders and top candidates are framed as "dowry" discussions—the size of the financial commitment that the institution provides to the candidate; not just in terms of compensation, but in other resources such as additional faculty positions, space, and financial resources.

The problem with "dowry" discussions is that they are unidirectional. Rather, negotiations could be better framed as mutual agreements upon which both the institution and individual agree. Researchers suggest that candidates want more than just an appropriate resource package (Fernández-Aráoz, Groysberg, & Nohria, 2009). Candidates also are looking for sincere expressions of commitment and concern from the dean and CEO about their motivations and long-term fit with the organization. No one wants to be subject to a "bait-and-switch" after several months into a new position.

Candidate Experiences During the Process

The impressions that candidates form from one or more experiences during the recruitment process may play a determining role in the acceptance or rejection of an offer out of hand. In our experience, candidates' reasons for declining a position offer have included the following:

Chapter Digest

Candidates are looking for sincere expressions of commitment and concern. No one wants to be subject to a bait-and-switch after several months into a new position.

To understand the mutual commitments between organization and the top candidate, detailed letters of offer may include:

* Complete descriptions of reporting relationships and responsibilities
* Precise role of the position in the governance structures of medical school, hospital, practice plan, etc.
* Specific expectations of performance and affect on compensation
* Institutional and department/unit support to meet goals
* Description of periodic review to ascertain "delivery of promises" by all parties.

(See pages 51–53.)

"Negotiations could be better framed as mutual agreements upon which both the institution and individual agree."

- Friction between members of the search committee exhibited during the interview process, such as argumentative exchanges that made the candidate and other committee members uncomfortable
- Conflicting opinions among key stakeholders about the nature of the unit, its goals, the expectations of the dean or CEO, and past events—as shared with the candidate in separate conversations with department members or potential colleagues
- Dissatisfied or disgruntled comments made informally or casually that indicate organizational conflict or lack of cohesion
- Personality differences with one or more of candidate's most important future peers
- The candidate's inherent disagreement with the strategic direction, scope, or influence of the position itself

The Final Recruitment Process

In the final "push" to recruit the first-choice candidate to the organization, institutional leaders should be able to articulate the following items:

- The nature and vision of the institution and the department, center, or unit
- The match between what the institution needs and what the candidate has to offer
- The positive aspects of being a member of the institution's leadership team
- Reasons why this particular position is interesting and challenging
- The nature of the relationship with the dean or CEO, the opportunities for mentorship, and future leadership development
- A realistic and straightforward preview of the job and its challenges
- Information that distinguishes this position from others currently available in the field
- A definition of available institutional and departmental resources
- An understanding of the candidate's comfort level with contractual arrangements, including length of appointment, criteria for performance, provision for review and evaluation, mission performance-related rewards and compensation, and conditions of termination

Furthermore, institutional leaders should agree on the following issues prior to the final recruitment:
- A clear definition of the upper limits of resources available for negotiation
- An agreement among key leaders on how to deal with the "reluctant candidate"
- An understanding by all key negotiators of the social dimension involved in the particular candidate's recruitment (e.g., two-career issues, children's educational needs, etc.)

Innovations at Work:
A Team Approach to Final Negotiations

At the University of Wisconsin School of Medicine and Public Health, the dean handles final negotiations with candidates for chair positions in consultation with a team of administrative leaders (such as the associate dean of administration, associate dean of research, and associate dean of fiscal affairs) who have knowledge of the available resources. Prior to initiating negotiations, the dean asks each associate dean to provide the details of what could be available from their respective area (money, space, positions, etc.) and uses that information in the negotiation. All of these individuals also review the final offer letter. For clinical chairs, the CEO of the hospital and CEO of the physician practice plan are also consulted and provide an appropriate letter of support that is included with the offer letter. The feedback and edits on offer letters are done via e-mail with tight response times.

The Detailed Letter of Appointment

Over the last decade, many academic medical centers have transformed the use of letters of appointments to specifically stipulate the institution's commitment to the individual and the individual's responsibilities to the institution. See Appendix 12 for a template letter of appointment.

Today, appointment letters typically state the responsibilities of the position and contain a formal business plan that projects the annual distribution of salary and research support over the first few years following appointment. The letter identifies an annual review process and ties salary to performance in specified areas. Newer approaches also include the assessment of the "impact of activities" in addition to quantitative measures of performance.

While the sample letters in the appendices are focused on faculty appointments, many leaders of academic medical centers take a similar approach for the appointment of department chairs, center directors, and other leadership positions. Many leaders work on multiple drafts of the appointment letter with the candidate of choice until both parties are satisfied with the expectations and conditions. Said one medical school dean who takes this approach:

> Ultimately, my success in getting the best people is related to a sense of trust—and that comes through having very frank discussions in the recruitment process. With the final candidate, we spend a lot of time talking about vision. I try to bring in the candidate as my partner. We work a draft [appointment] document together through a lot of back and forth—that gives me an opportunity to see if we're on the same page.

Such a constructive appointment letter should be revisited during the annual reviews to ascertain the "delivery of promises" by both parties and to provide a platform to assess the performance of the department chair, center director, or other leader.

Most department chairs and center directors do not have contracts in the traditional sense. University attorneys advise many deans that a detailed letter of appointment, agreed to by both parties, is an equivalent document. Of course, a contract does not ensure understanding between two parties. For example, despite having very detailed

"Many academic medical centers have transformed the use of letters of appointments to specifically stipulate the institution's commitment to the individual and the individual's responsibilities to the institution."

traditional contracts, "about one-fifth of university presidents felt that they did not have a clear understanding of some aspect of the campus or the job at the time they took the position." (American Council on Education, 2000, p. 3). The detailed appointment letter, reviewed by and agreed to by both the hiring authority and candidate, can help achieve congruence between expectations and opportunities.

The Detailed Letter of Offer

- Full titles of position and specific reporting relationships and responsibilities:

    Description of the reporting line to dean or hospital CEO, and definition of other direct (dual) reporting lines (if they exist); e.g., to the director of the practice plan, hospital CEO, department chair(s), or to an interdisciplinary institute or center

- Academic rank and tenure status, with financial implications of tenure status, if any

- Administrative appointments. Define the precise role of the position in the governance structures of the parent university (if any), the medical school, the university hospitals, the practice plan, and the VA system (if applicable)

- Date of appointment. Specify expectations for dates of full activity in each mission

- Personal financial compensation. Specify expectations of performance and of dates of full activity in each of the criteria related to base salary; and institutional, departmental, and individual performance criteria related to possible incentive salary. Statement of institutional benefits: insurance, retirement, etc.

Continued on next page.

The Detailed Letter of Offer (cont.)

- Relocation cost reimbursement

- Institutional and departmental negotiated support:
    i. Financial support from the dean's office, and specific criteria for the mission-related use of that support
    ii. Departmental academic and research space. Criteria and timetable for retention of this space, and for the gain of additional space
    iii. Faculty positions available: salary support of additional positions, start-up package support from dean for new faculty hires
    iv. Financial support for residents (and number of residents)
    v. Financial support from hospital for clinical administrative functions of physician faculty

- Legally acceptable "success-sharing" program with hospital

- Dean/CEO's expectations of all institutional leaders

- Dean/CEO's expectations of this particular position—recitation of leader's vision for this role and program

- Teaching hospital CEO's expectations of the clinical department

- Term of appointment

- Mechanisms of review and intervals of review

- Conditions of termination

- Mentorship and coaching opportunities and resources

10 Successful Leadership Transitions

The decision has been made; the offer has been accepted. Is the process over? No. The search and recruitment phase may end, but the transition process is only beginning. This getting-to-know-you phase—the manner in which the new leader and the organization are introduced to each other—is important. Gilmore defines the transition process as the time when the leader, the current staff, and the institution

> develop an understanding of one another's expectations and fashion their new working relationships…The orientation period may also be the time of working through the loss of the prior leader. The appointing authority often disengages too quickly once the search has landed a candidate, rather than making the additional investment necessary to ensure that the new leader builds effective working relationships upward, downwards, and sideways. (Gilmore, 1993, p. 6)

Each new leader will make changes. He or she will face a number of people who resist such change. New chairs, center directors, and other leaders need support from institutional executives, their peers, and their faculty supporters to help them navigate these changes, to deal with individuals who resist change, and to help their organizations heal from the loss and fear that accompanies change and transition (Souba & McFadden, 2009).

Sessa and colleagues (1998) found that, among multiple variables, the relationships that executives had with subordinates were most clearly linked to early outcomes of success and failure. Their research showed that successful executives had more positive transitional support than did unsuccessful leaders. They also found that externally selected executives more likely had a "grace period" of several months. In contrast, a greater proportion of internally selected executives were evaluated during this early phase, and their performance was judged more harshly than their externally selected peers.

How to Bring a New Leader on Board

The process of "on-boarding" for new department chairs, center directors, and other leaders will vary depending on many factors: whether the new hire is external or internal, whether the unit is in a period of stability or crisis, and the culture of the unit and the organization. Despite these variations, one commonality applies to the transition process as much as it applied to the search process: you need a plan.

It is the hiring authority's responsibility to ensure that the new hire has an on-boarding plan, but the search committee chair has an important role to play as well, as she or he will be among the people whom the new leader knows best. The organization's human resources department can be invaluable in providing helpful transition assistance, such as contacts for local childcare, banks, faith communities, schools, and other local services.

Chapter Digest

While the process of on-boarding will vary from one organization to the next, and from one position to the next, one commonality will apply: you need a plan.

The ways academic medical centers welcome new leaders can include:

* Help in developing a peer network
* Mentoring
* Assistance in planning a department/unit retreat
* Assistance in strategic planning
* Leadership development
* Executive coaching
* Concierge program
* Services for spouse/partner/family
(See pages 56–57.)

"One commonality applies to the transition process as much as it applied to the search process: you need a plan."

Components of On-boarding at Medical Schools and Teaching Hospitals

The ways academic medical centers welcome new leaders into the community and orient them to their positions can include:

- Help in developing a peer network (often, the search committee chair can be effective in this role)
- Mentoring, formally or informally
- Assistance and resources to plan a department or unit retreat
- Assistance (internal or external) in strategic planning
- Leadership development, such as a national program like the AAMC's Executive Development Seminar for Associate Deans and Department Chairs
- Executive coaching
- An "operational orientation" to the few but critical systems, processes, and policies used in day-to-day work
- Concierge program, such as assistance with childcare, pets, banking, personal services, schools, and faith communities; "concierge-level" service in completing benefits process
- Services for spouse/partner/family
- A series of scheduled short-term and informally structured "check-in" meetings or conversations to make the assurance of ongoing support explicit

"Creating a welcoming climate is similar to recruiting a new leader: it requires a continuum beginning with recruitment and ending with a succession plan."

Creating a Welcoming Climate

Different leaders have varying needs as they join a new organization. A network of peers can be helpful to any new leader. In the case of new leaders who are women; members of underrepresented minorities; or members of the gay, bisexual, lesbian, or transgendered community, creation of a welcoming climate is imperative.

For these groups, developing a network of peers may be challenging. For example, although women now comprise 49 percent of medical school graduates, they only make up only 34 percent of all faculty, 17 percent of full professors, and 14 percent of department chairs (AAMC, 2008).

Mahoney et al. (2008) speak of the unique mentoring needs of minority faculty across all ranks. Minority department chairs and other organizational leaders may also have similar needs for mentoring and support. Because few minority faculty attain leadership roles in academic medicine, fewer role models with similar backgrounds are available to these new leaders.

Likewise, support for members of the GLBT community makes good sense. Dohrenwend (2009) argues "GLBT faculty and students are not provided with a safe and equal environment in which to work and learn . . . Medicine cannot fulfill its obligation to GLBT patients, students, and faculty without a considerable and determined commitment to change." Recruiting, appointing, and retaining GLBT leaders requires the creation of a climate of acceptance and support—tolerance alone is not enough. Creating a welcoming climate is similar to recruiting a new leader: it requires a continuum beginning with recruitment and ending with a succession plan (Figure 10.1).

Figure 10.1
The Continuum of Creating a Welcoming Climate

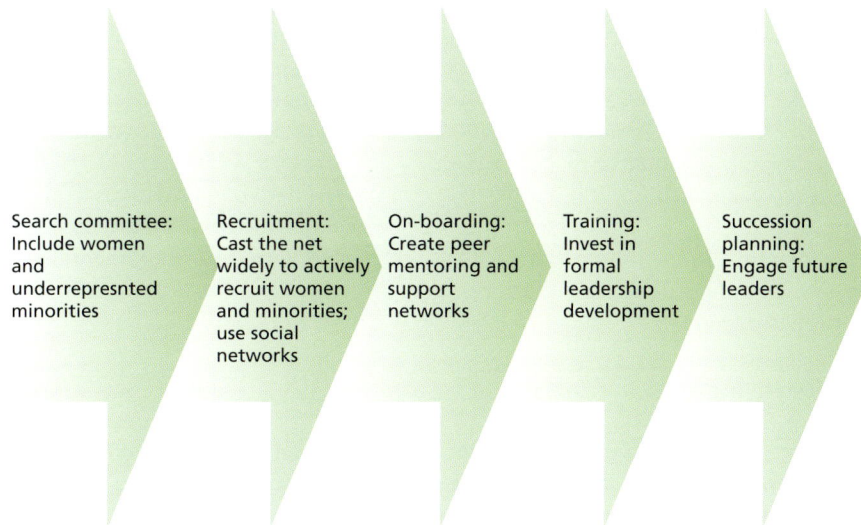

| Search committee: Include women and underrepresnted minorities | Recruitment: Cast the net widely to actively recruit women and minorities; use social networks | On-boarding: Create peer mentoring and support networks | Training: Invest in formal leadership development | Succession planning: Engage future leaders |

Five Ways to Fail as a New Leader

As new leaders come into a new organizational culture, and as institutions prepare to welcome and assimilate them, all involved can learn as much from *unsuccessful* leadership transitions as from successful ones. Why do some transitions go awry?

1. New leaders ignore the culture

Ignoring or failing to understand the organizational culture has been the undoing of many new leaders. This is especially true for persons entering organizations from outside as the new leader. Even if the leader has a successful track record in a similar position elsewhere, moving to another organization means the leader is "new" to the organization. This pitfall can apply to a leader who has been promoted within an organization; in the new role, these internal candidates will be perceived differently by their peers. In fact, when they become the new leader, it's likely they will no longer be regarded as a peer—they will now be regarded as "a boss."

Simply put, organizational culture is "the way we do things around here." Leaders, whether new to the organization, new to the leadership role, or both, must consider the consequences of any decision within the context of "the way things are done around here." Sometimes, new leaders fall prey to making "the right decision in the wrong culture." In other words, engaging in what might have been effective action in her or his former role or organization is ineffective, at best, and dysfunctional at worst, in the context of the new leadership role or organization.

Sometimes the best advice for new leaders is: "Don't just do something, stand there." In other words, the impulse to act may be off-target. What worked in one's previous role or organization may not work in the new role or organization; rather, the best advice might be to wait until one has a better understanding of the culture before acting.

"Ignoring or failing to understand the organizational culture has been the undoing of many new leaders."

2. They focus too much attention on quick wins

Quick wins, sometimes referred to as "harvesting low-hanging fruit," allow new leaders to demonstrate early success and gain the confidence of those they lead. Sacrificing the long term in favor of quick wins may feel good—after all, everyone loves a winner. In fact, we love ourselves when we win, and healthy self-love is a part of effective leadership. Unfortunately, too much focus on short-term, easy wins may overshadow lurking long-term, complex problems that may soon become urgent (Van Buren & Saperstone, 2009). The 2008 crisis in the banking industry is a good example of short-term "irrational exuberance" where quick wins led many to believe that a downturn in the housing market was impossible. This type of mentality ignores long-term, complex problems, which can have dire consequences if they are not effectively confronted.

3. Leaders stop listening and start squawking

New leaders are often plagued by a tendency to talk too much. In his illuminating fable, *Squawk!*, Travis Bradberry (2008) describes this tendency to swoop in, squawk loudly, and dump orders as "seagull management." Although well-intentioned, this behavior isn't helpful. Some of this tendency is probably born of anxiety, but too much talk often originates in the belief that leading is all about making decisions. Effective leadership requires so much more. A leader may believe she or he was selected because of her or his history of making good decisions. This may be true, but making decisions as an individual is different from making decisions as a leader. Showcasing one's brilliance as a leader by offering immediate solutions is risky.

> *"New leaders are often plagued by a tendency to talk too much."*

Part of leading is about learning to listen to the wisdom of others. Understanding the diverse perspectives of others leads to better decision making. A rule of thumb is to *be sure you are listening twice as much as you are talking*. After all, we have two ears—but only one mouth.

4. New leaders ignore conflict

Ignoring conflict can greatly enhance the chance of failure. New leaders often hold the mistaken belief that ignoring conflict will make it go away. Some remain silent hoping people will forget about the issue. One of the facts of a life of leadership is you cannot avoid conflict. You can repress it, suppress it, ignore it, or postpone it, but you cannot avoid it. Sooner or later, leaders will have to face it—and even then, they may not be able to resolve it.

This behavior is often deeply rooted in the cultural myth of the "rugged individualist" who attributes success to determination and hard work. We hear vestiges of this belief in the lyrics of pop songs ("I did it my way") and in the adage "If you want it done right, do it yourself." Ignoring conflict is often a sign of a leader's immaturity or narcissism. Believing conflict will "just go away" is not only a delusion—for some leaders, it is an enduring fantasy. Ultimately, living this fantasy will result in leadership failure as conflicts endure and, in some cases, escalate over time.

5. They create a strategic plan that is neither

Many new leaders are very keen on engaging in a period of strategic planning. Too often, many persons in the organization invest weeks or months in the planning process only to emerge with a strategic plan that contains no real strategy. Likewise, it isn't really a plan—it is a statement of what the leader aspires to leave as her legacy. Too often, the commitment of resources is not included as part of the plan. Unless there is a clear statement of strategic intent tied to a commitment of resources with identified sources, then it is neither strategic, nor is it a plan. The naive belief "If it is a good enough idea, the resources will be found" will be perpetuated.

"Unless there is a clear statement of strategic intent tied to a commitment of resources with identified sources, then it is neither strategic, nor is it a plan."

11 Continuous Learning

A 2009 survey of medical school deans about leadership recruitment practices unearthed a paradox (Mallon & Corrice, 2009). Among the 90 respondents to the survey, over 85 percent of deans were satisfied or very satisfied with the ability of the finalists in department chair and center director searches to meet the most pressing needs of the position. Yet when deans were asked to name top recruitment challenges, the most common concern was how to find candidates who possess leadership and management competencies and how to ensure a good fit between the candidate and the institutional culture.

On the one hand, deans were highly satisfied with the leaders they had recruited for a *specific* position. On the other hand, they noted anxiety with finding candidates with the right leadership competencies *in general.*

This paradox may speak to the need for continuous learning and refinement of the leadership search and recruitment process in academic medicine. While organizational leaders appear satisfied with the candidates they have before them, there is still a hunger for a broader and deeper pool of candidates with demonstrated leadership competencies, including an understanding of the demands of leadership, an appreciation of organizational culture, and the courage and skills to manage organizational change.

So no matter how well (or poorly) any search unfolds, academic medical centers can always improve the process and outcomes of the search. In some areas—such as the ability to attract women and minorities to leadership positions—medical schools and teaching hospitals can surely improve their performance.

Continuous Learning from the Search Process

Organizations can learn and improve over time by reviewing and evaluating the search process itself. A key associate or vice dean or human resources professional can coordinate this learning cycle. While the search committee chair would be an important participant in the "after action review," he or she should not lead the evaluation process.

Some academic medical centers ask candidates to provide feedback on their campus visit. Of course, the timing of such feedback is a delicate issue. Candidates who remain under consideration for the position may not be open and honest with legitimate concerns for fear of appearing critical. On the other hand, one might worry that if the organization waits to elicit feedback until after the search is over, rejected finalists may be *overly* critical of the visit. While this timing might be a worry, we believe that candidates who are treated with hospitality, warmth, and professionalism will be respectful and helpful with their feedback, even if they were ultimately not chosen for the position.

For an example of a candidate visit feedback instrument used by the University of Arizona College of Medicine, see Appendix 13.

Toward an Integrated System of Recruitment, Expectations, Evaluation, Development, and Rewards

Judith McLaughlin, a scholar on university presidential searches at the Harvard Graduate School of Education, once conducted a wonderful study (Biebuyck & Mallon, 2003). One year after initial presidential appointments, she interviewed the university president, members of the search committee, and various faculty members, students, and trustees to learn whether the appointment succeeded and whether the incumbent had delivered what the institution thought it was seeking.

This study was thought provoking for two reasons. By asking such questions and facing the answers, institutions can learn about their organizational successes and failures. Many institutions would be afraid to hear the answers! Second, the underlining philosophy of the study suggests a direct connection between appointment expectations and future evaluation that is rarely made. Yet, the recruitment, development, evaluation, and compensation of leaders are inextricably linked.

Relatively few institutions—companies, universities, or academic medical centers—create processes and practices so that these functions work together seamlessly. For example, how many academic medical centers tie search criteria to evaluation standards as McLauglin's study did? One way for medical schools to do this would be to place several members of the original search committee on the new leader's annual evaluation process.

Organizations need to create explicit linkages among selection criteria, appointment guidelines, well-defined expectations and responsibilities, professional development, clear evaluation processes, and thoughtful reward structures to form a coherent, comprehensive system of employment (see Figure 11.1).

When expectations and responsibilities are explicitly acknowledged in the selection process and when performance evaluation criteria reinforce those expectations and responsibilities, academic medical centers can create coherent, integrated systems for successful performance and behaviors—not just for leaders, but for all faculty, staff, residents, and students.

It is our hope that *Finding Top Talent* facilitates a dialogue among medical school deans, hospital executives, chairs and center directors, search committee chairs and members, and faculty to discuss recruitment practices that work and improve those that don't.

Continuous Learning

Figure 11.1
An Integrated System for Leadership Selection, Development, Evaluation, and Rewards

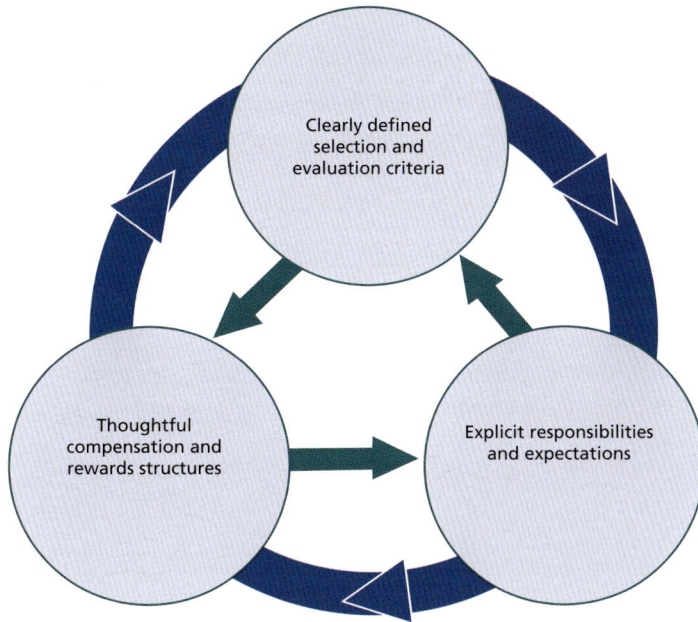

Appendices

Appendix 1
Position Description
Associate Dean for Leadership Development
Medical College of Georgia School of Medicine

The strategic foci of recruiting, developing, and retaining senior leaders are constants in an Academic Health Center and are essential not only to growth, but also to stability through succession planning. Acknowledging talent as the primary asset in a knowledge-driven enterprise, the SOM organizational capability strategy links "make," or talent development activities with "buy" search/selection activities via a dedicated senior leadership position.

Position Overview: Associate Dean, Leadership Development

The Associate Dean for Leadership reports directly to the Dean, School of Medicine/Senior Vice President for Health Affairs. Organizationally, this position resides in the School of Medicine.

In consultation with the SOM Dean and supported by the Chief of Staff, the Associate Dean for Leadership Development is the primary steward of SOM talent acquisition strategies and has executive responsibility for developing, implementing, evaluating, and refining processes that support and enable organizational capability and success.

Qualifications and Personal Characteristics

The Associate Dean for Leadership Development will possess comprehensive knowledge and experience spanning all tripartite mission components of the SOM, including education, research, and patient care; and will have the degree/comparable degree of MD or PhD. S/he will be an incumbent department chair or program principal who has achieved all of the following outcomes in his/her primary academic unit:

- Superior academic, clinical, and operational performance as evidenced by quantitative metrics;
- Development and implementation of a successful program of faculty development;
- Unit stability and growth; and
- Development and empowerment of secondary leadership depth that enables continuity of day-to-day operations in the absence of the department chair/program principal.

S/he must be a respected leader who possesses the depth of character and interpersonal skills to:

- Support department chairs, program principals, and academic administrators in implementing strategies to recruit/retain and continuously develop a faculty that is talented, productive, interdependent, and fulfilled;
- Enable successful management and closure of difficult human interactions and organizational dynamics, in both individual and group settings;
- Credibly represent the Dean and the SOM to local, regional, and national organizations; and actively engage in strategic activities of high impact and visibility.

S/he will discharge his/her duties with:

- A style that is inclusive but decisive; and
- An understanding of the critical role of search and selection; tempered not only by compassion, but also by a sense of humor.

Principal Duties and Responsibilities

The Associate Dean for Leadership Development has executive responsibility for developing, implementing, evaluating, and continuously improving a comprehensive SOM strategy for leadership recruitment, development, and retention that is:

- Driven by data, innovation, and inquiry;
- Intuitive to both risk and nascent leadership potential;
- Successful as measured by quantitative and qualitative performance metrics;
- Characterized by "best practices"; and
- Aligned with local, regional, and national strategic initiatives

Portfolio Dimensions: Leadership Search and Selection

Represent and serve as primary counsel to the SOM Dean in strategies and processes for leadership recruitment:

- Advise the Dean on strategic composition of leadership search and selection committees:
- Serve as senior leadership anchor for all SOM search and selection committee processes. Chair or co-chair academic search committees to:
  - Identify and select 'Best in Class' leaders
  - Ensure accountability of committee and committee members, and credibility of processes
  - Develop leadership potential of co-chairs and committee members to build depth and breadth of institutional talent pool
  - Enable organizational learning and continuous improvement of processes.
- Considering needs unique to each leadership position, provide strategic direction in assessing, selecting, and engaging executive search firms. Serve as the institutional liaison to engaged firm.
- Collaborate with the Chief of staff to develop, implement, evaluate and continuously refine search communication processes, including:
  - Candidate briefings and materials representative of SOM missions and strategic direction; and
  - Ongoing communications appropriate to various internal and external stakeholders and constituencies.

- Provide design consultation and oversight to post-search evaluation processes toward continuous process improvement and organizational learning; direct responsive refinement of search and selection processes as indicated.
- Represent the Dean and SOM to internal (e.g., the University System of Georgia) and external (e.g., the AAMC) constituencies for strategic leadership search and selection initiatives.

Portfolio Dimensions: Leadership Development

Represent and serve as primary counsel to the SOM Dean in strategies and processes to identify and develop faculty with leadership potential. In collaboration with the Chief of Staff and Executive Associate Dean for Administration, develop and link initiatives for support staff.

- Through liaison with department chairs and program principals; and through other internal linkages and assessment mechanisms, develop and maintain an awareness of faculty leadership potential. In collaboration with the Chief of Staff and Executive Associate Dean for Administration, identify, develop, and track the institutional talent pool.
- Anticipate, understand, and respond to organizational needs. Maintain a connection with and awareness of internal and external environments toward synthesis of leadership development programming needs.
- Provide executive leadership for implementation and evaluation of programming.
- Represent the Dean and SOM to internal (e.g., the University System of Georgia) and external (e.g., the AAMC) constituencies for strategic leadership development initiatives.

General Leadership Responsibilities

- As a member of School of Medicine senior leadership team, develop, support, and advocate for a shared School of Medicine vision and accountability:
    - Participate in team-based decision making processes; support decisions and actions of the School of Medicine senior leadership team, as well as decisions and actions of fellow team members
    - Support an environment that recognizes and rewards excellence: promote a positive culture of institutional excellence, achievement, and pride for all School of Medicine students, faculty, and staff; and by their extended families

- Support the Dean in planning, executing, and evaluating School of Medicine strategies, programs, policies, and operations.
    - Model responsible stewardship of institutional resources in a manner consistent with the strategic goals of the SOM;
    - Ensure that relevant SOM policies and practices foster excellence, equity, and diversity

- Enhance the image of the School of Medicine as an institution engaged with medical leadership initiatives regionally and nationally by maintaining a presence at local, regional, and national activities of relevance (e.g. AAMC).
- Support for credible philanthropic initiatives and programs linked to the institution's development strategy.

Appendix 2
A Model Search Committee Code of Conduct

Preamble

You have been asked to serve on this search committee because our organization has a high degree of trust in you. As a search committee member, you will have access to information that is otherwise confidential, and you will assume an important role in the process to select new leaders for the organization.

Therefore, it is imperative that you use the highest standards of ethical and professional conduct to protect the integrity of the process and the integrity of each and every candidate. Your signature on this document attests to your understanding of and commitment to maintaining the highest standards of ethical and professional conduct.

Standards

As a member of this search committee, I agree to uphold the following principles:

> **Honesty:** I agree to fully disclose current and former relationships with candidates. I will fully reveal any real or potential conflicts of interest in the relationships of committee members and candidates. I agree to correct any inaccuracies of commission or omission for which I am responsible.

> **Respect for all persons:** I will respect other search committee members and all potential candidates and candidates. I agree to maintain civility in all transactions with other committee members, search professionals, search support personnel, potential candidates, and candidates. Further, I agree to attend all meetings unless excused. I pledge to arrive on time and fully participate in the committee activities. I will respect all candidates and participants in the search process across the wide range of diverse backgrounds, temperaments, generations, and orientations.

> **Privacy:** I agree to maintain appropriate boundaries and will not go outside of the formal process to obtain information about candidates, will not intrude into private lives of candidates, and will not participate in gossip about the process or about candidates or others involved in the search process.

> **Confidentiality:** I will keep private all information about search committee proceedings, identity of potential candidates or candidates, origin of candidates, and all other search-related discussions, even after the search is completed. I acknowledge that the search committee chair is the only person authorized to speak on behalf of the committee.

In addition to adhering to the principles stated above, I agree to participate in and responsibly discharge all of the assignments requested of me as a committee member. I will put the best interests of the organization ahead of my personal interests, and will not allow those personal interests to interfere with my duties as a committee member.

_____   _____
Name/Signature   Date

Appendix 3
Responsibilities of Department Chairs
at the University of Wisconsin (UW) School of Medicine and Public Health
(SMPH)

SMPH department chairs are expected to provide strong leadership to ensure that the following responsibilities are achieved/fulfilled:

1. Chairs are responsible for establishing and maintaining the appropriate balance and high quality of the academic department in all areas of department's mission: teaching, research and service. They are accountable for medical student education within the department and for cooperating with interdisciplinary programs, established and proposed, with other departments both within and outside of the SMPH.

2. Chairs are responsible for accomplishing department-related objectives of the SMPH Strategic Plan, for achieving selected performance targets established by the dean with the chair, and for serving on SMPH and UW committees and panels.

3. As service chiefs of UW Hospital and Clinics, the Chairs are responsible to the Hospital CEO, or his/her designee, to establish departmental objectives to meet the hospital's strategic and annual operating plan, assure sufficient clinical coverage to meet the hospitals' clinical services needs, and to provide leadership to meet JCAHO and other regulatory requirements of the leadership and medical staff standards, assure outstanding clinical outcomes, and achieve high levels of referring physician and patient satisfaction.

4. In accordance with university policies and the SMPH diversity goals and objectives, chairs are responsible for proactively supporting recruitment of female and ethnic minority faculty to meet SMPH diversity goals. They are expected to assure a gender-friendly environment and gender pay equity for all faculty.

5. Chairs are responsible for facilitating the career development of junior faculty within the department. This includes providing sufficient start-up resources for all junior faculty and establishing and implementing an appropriate mentor policy. Chairs are also responsible for ensuring that the executive committee accomplishes timely performance appraisals, promotion reviews, and post-tenure reviews.

6. In addition, chairs of clinical departments are responsible for ensuring that clinical faculty are appointed to the appropriate track and that all junior faculty and the tracking process are reviewed periodically. Chairs of clinical departments generally serve as Chief of Service for the University of Wisconsin Hospital and Clinics (UWHC) and are responsible for directing graduate medical education (residency programs).

7. In concurrence with the executive committee, chairs are accountable for planning, managing, and effectively monitoring all fiscal resources and activities of the department.

Chairs are also responsible for managing and effectively using all space assigned by the SMPH and the UWHC.

These guidelines are intended to support SMPH department chairs in their leadership roles.

Appendix 4
Recommended Steps for a Successful Search

Our intent is not to impose a single, uniform procedure but to outline general steps and to describe good practices.

Step 1: Organize internal (including self-study) and/or external review of department, center, or unit.

Step 2: Medical school and teaching hospital leaders, using review reports and other available information, decide on future direction of department, discipline, center, or unit. Options may include:
- Continue mission and direction
- Change mission and direction
- Change unit name
- Combine unit with another in the school or incorporate functions within a center
- "Outsource" the current responsibilities
- Close the unit

Step 3: Institutional leaders decide, based on the history, reviews and desired future directions, on the major qualities to be sought in the new leader.

Step 4: In the event leaders decide to continue with the existing structure, initiate the search and selection process for a new leader.

Step 5: Dean, CEO, or hiring authority selects chair of search committee.

Step 6: Committee chair negotiates appropriate administrative infrastructure for search committee.

Step 7: Dean/CEO and search committee chair decide whether to hire a search consultant.

Step 8: Dean or hiring authority, with advice from search committee chair, teaching hospital CEO, and other key advisors, makes search committee membership appointments.

Step 9: Hiring authority announces to the internal institutional community that a national search for new leadership will be conducted.

Step 10: Committee chair, together with search committee administrator and dean's administrator, identifies and announces date for first meeting of search committee.

Step 11: Committee chair prepares agenda for first meeting, which will include, at a minimum:
- Dean/CEO sharing results of departmental review as appropriate and decision about the future role and direction of the department and discipline.
- Dean's charge to the committee, which should include and emphasize the characteristics to be sought by the committee in leading candidates.

- Dean's "general sense" of significant additional resources to be made available to a successful candidate.
- Dean's emphasis of the fact that the search committee is advisory to the dean and will not, at any time, function as a selection committee.
- Dean's reassurance to committee members that no candidate will be considered who has not entered the process through consideration by, and on the recommendation of, the search committee.
- Dean's specific timetable for various search stages to the committee
- Dean's instruction to committee on desired outcome of search stage (i.e., the number of finalists to be presented by the search committee and the composition of the finalist group).
- Dean's instructions to the committee on critical importance of absolute confidentiality of all committee deliberations.
- Dean's emphasis of the importance of search for future of institution.
- Dean's emphasis that members of committee have been selected for their institutional perspective and expertise, and not as representatives of any campus group.
- Dean's emphasis of the role of the committee chair as the sole spokesperson for the committee in all matters related to the search.
- If the decision to hire a search consultant has been made, the dean should, in the presence of the consultant, outline the precise role the consultant will play and emphasize the primacy of the search committee in the process.
- In the case of a search for a chair of a clinical department, it is constructive to invite the teaching hospital CEO to address the committee at this stage in order to ensure that the committee members understand the hospital's expectations for the department.
- It is advisable for the university affirmative action officer to address the committee at this first meeting, to explain the committee's responsibilities in conducting a proactive search and following university guidelines.
- Committee chair repeats essential confidentiality of entire process to the committee.
- Chair announces dates for regular meetings.
- Chair distributes information on department or unit, and previous departmental/unit reports.
- Chair appoints sub-group of committee to work on position description and advertisement for chair, to report back at next meeting.
  - o If partnering with a search consultant, the consultant will play the major role in the construction of the detailed position description. While this document is particularly intended for serious candidates, an abstract can be used to construct the advertisements and the cover letter to nominees from the search committee chair.

- Committee discusses small group of national leaders who will be asked by the chair to act as confidential advisors and "mentors to the committee chair" throughout the search process.
- Committee discusses "the competition" (i.e., the other searches currently active in the same area at other institutions).

Step 12: Committee determines placement of advertisements in appropriate national (and possibly international) journals, academic news publications, and Web sites of relevant professional associations. The text of these advertisements may be tailored from a template for major leadership positions at the institution.

Step 13: The committee identifies individuals to whom letters will be sent by committee chair announcing search and requesting nominations, such as:
- Deans of all U.S. and Canadian medical schools
- Chairs of all departments of discipline in question in North America
- Chairs of closely related disciplines
- Center directors in related areas
- Internal academic constituency (i.e., chairs and faculty in medical school and teaching hospital and residents of relevant department)

Step 14: Chair of search committee makes important calls to begin to establish a "network" for the search:
- To chairs of recently completed searches in the same area
- To the small group of identified nationally recognized leaders in the discipline or area, who will serve as advisors and mentors. The group of leaders should specifically include women and minority leaders in the discipline. (During these initial calls, a significant group of leading candidates is usually gathered.)

Step 15: Search committee administrator establishes log for recording nominations, letters sent to candidates, replies received from candidates, curricula vitae received, and committee actions.

Step 16: Search committee administrator sends acknowledgment letters to persons who have submitted nominations.

Step 17: Search committee agrees on evaluation criteria based on the requirements for the position and constructs candidate evaluation form and score sheet (or tailors from template). These criteria will be applied to all candidates.

Step 18: Search committee administrator drafts letters from committee chair to each nominee who submits curriculum vitae and who becomes an "active" candidate.

Step 19: Search committee chair reviews responses from nominees and plans calls to those previously identified "leading" candidates who have not responded or who have declined to become candidates.

Step 20: Search committee identifies "short list" of candidates to be invited for first interview. (Ideally, search committee chair should make initial inquiries to national leaders about this list of candidates prior to issuing the first invitation.)

Step 21: Search committee decides if the initial interviews occur during a "full-scale" visit to the campus or will the committee travel to a neutral location and interview all the candidates on the same day?

Step 22: Search committee carefully develops a list of core questions based on criteria by which the candidates are to be evaluated. The committee plans precisely which committee member will pose each question to candidates.

Step 23: If candidates visit the campus for first interviews, the search committee chair has to decide who will be invited to meet with the candidate. The first visit should be a "less intense" and shorter interview schedule than a second visit will be. Spouses and family members should not be invited to accompany candidate on this visit. Appointments with realtors, school principals, etc., are also not appropriate for this visit.

Step 24: "In-house" search coordinator, associate dean for faculty affairs or diversity, or human resources professional meets with the search committee and all interviewers about effective interviewing techniques, including how to ask behavioral questions.

Step 25: Written evaluations are gathered from each individual search committee member and campus members who interviewed the candidates.

Step 26: The search committee decides on two to five finalists to invite for the second interview. The dean and CEO should be included in this interview schedule. It is also appropriate to invite the spouse/partner on this occasion. For dual-career couples, arrange for the spouse/partner to explore professional opportunities at this stage.

Step 27: The search committee chair must give very close personal attention to the subtleties of the interview schedule for this visit. Department or center faculty, residents, and students should be included. This is the opportunity to ensure that no key player or constituency is omitted from a formal invitation to meet with the candidate.

Step 28: Search committee decides whether to have candidate give a seminar or interact at a "town meeting-style" social gathering with the department, center, or unit. Social interactions with other institutional leaders are also important in making final assessments.

Step 29: Search committee reviews written evaluations of all who met candidate on second visit and decides on list of finalists.

Step 30: Search committee chair or designee makes calls to national and local colleagues familiar with each of these finalist candidates. Information should be gathered about demonstrated leadership abilities; vision; flexibility; national standing as an academic, educator, and clinician; service; collegiality; and interpersonal abilities. Calls should be made to colleagues, administrators, nurses, residents, students, and those who report to the candidate, in addition to leaders and superiors. The same person should perform these reference checks using a similar set of prepared questions.

Step 31: Search committee reviews results of calls made during "due diligence" processes, and decides on final list to present to dean/CEO or hiring authority. The final list should include a comparative analysis of the relative strengths and weaknesses of each finalist.

Step 32: The dean or CEO now contacts additional national references (e.g., deans, hospital leaders, department chairs, or center directors who the hiring authority knows personally) in a further, and often crucial, evaluation of the finalists. The hiring authority also might conduct a reverse site visit to each of the finalists.

Step 33: Dean decides whether to invite finalists (or a subset of the group) back for third visit for final assessment or whether to make selection of her top choice at this stage.

Step 34: Upon acceptance of the offer, close-off letters should be sent to unsuccessful candidates.

Appendix 5
Engaging a Search Firm

Suggestions when hiring an external search firm:

- Decide in advance who will be the points of contact for the firm's principal
    - In most cases, the chair of the search committee will be the primary contact. If your organization also has an in-house search expert, the search chair and this individual must be clear about who serves as primary contact.
    - In addition, identify the person who will be the administrative support liaison

- Be very clear about the costs, contract specifications, and fiscal expectations prior to signing a contract with the search firm
    - Consider a contract provision by which you withholding some percentage of final payment to the firm until after the hired candidate's third month of employment or appointment.

- The initial meeting with the firm's principal should include:
    - Introduction of the search chair or professional liaison to the organization
    - Introduction of the administrative coordinator
    - Review of any policies, processes, or practices that might be unusual
    - Full disclosure about the coverage of travel and accommodations costs for both the search firm principal and any candidates who come to campus
    - Review of limitation on travel or expense reimbursement, including a detailed list of which expenses are excluded (alcohol, gifts, etc.)
    - Discussion of project timelines and deliverables

Questions for the search firm

The following are some suggested questions for the firm's principal. (Note that firms may be reluctant to provide some of this information; press for answers, but respect confidentiality.)

1. How many active searches do you personally have underway? How many do you anticipate in your portfolio during the period of our search?
2. May I have references for the last three searches you have done, personally, for similar organizations (and similar positions, if possible)?
3. Does the firm have a limit on the number of unsuccessful attempts by any one of its candidates?
4. Has any candidate been represented by this firm for a continuous search process lasting more than 18 months? What are the circumstances?
5. What unusual or extraordinary methods does this firm use in active recruitment of women and underrepresented minorities?
6. Of the last seven placements by the firm for positions in academic medicine, how many are women, people of color, and differently abled? How many candidates in those categories has your firm presented for on site interviews in the past 18 months?
7. How, specifically, have you assembled your list of candidates for our position?

Appendix 6
Behavioral Interviewing Questions
Lehigh Valley Health Network

Leadership Management

1. How would you describe your leadership philosophy and style?
2. What would you suppose your subordinates feel are your strengths and shortcomings from their point of view?
3. In what ways might you want to modify your approach to dealing with subordinates?

Performance Management

1. Tell me about the performance management system you now use.
2. How effective have your methods for following up on delegated assignments been?
3. Tell me about accountability. What happens when people fail to perform?
4. What do you say or do when someone reporting to you has made a significant (serious, costly) mistake?

Team Building

1. How have you tried to build teamwork?
2. Which of your teams has been the biggest disappointment in terms of cohesiveness or effectiveness?

Problem Solving

1. Give me an example of your problem-solving ability.
2. How have you incorporated collaborative problem solving in your organization?

Accomplishments

1. What has been your most significant accomplishment in each of your past two or three positions?
2. How did your accomplishments affect your organization as a whole?
3. Can you tell me about your most significant team achievements in your positions? What was your actual role?

Vision

1. What is your vision for your personal position?
2. How was the vision developed?
3. How do you communicate your vision?

Change Leadership

1. In what specific ways have you changed an organization the most (in terms of direction, results, policies)?
2. What has been your approach to communicating change?

Self-Awareness

1. Have you gotten any sort of systematic or regular feedback (360 degree or otherwise) from direct reports, peers, supervisors, and if so, what did you learn?

2. What are the biggest mistakes you've made in the past 10 years, and what have you learned from them?
3. What are your principle developmental needs and what are your plans to deal with them?
4. What have been the most difficult criticisms for you to accept?

Adaptability

1. How have you changed during recent years?
2. What sorts of organizational changes have you found easiest and most difficult to accept?
3. When have you been so firm people considered you stubborn and inflexible?

Stress Management

1. What sort of mood swings do you experience—how high are the highs, how low are the lows, and why?
2. Describe yourself in terms of emotional control? What sorts of things irritate you the most or get you down?
3. How many times have you "lost your cool" in the past couple of months?
4. Describe a situation in which you were the most angry you have been in years?

Initiative

1. What actions would you take in the first weeks, should you join our organization?
2. What sort of obstacles have you faced in your present position, and what did you do?
3. Who have been your major career influences, and why?

Organization/Planning

1. How well organized are you? What do you do to be organized, and what, if anything, do you feel you ought to do to be better organized?
2. Describe a complex challenge you have had coordinating a project.
3. If I were to talk with secretaries you have had during the past several years, how would they describe your strengths and weaker points with respect to personal organization, communication, attention to detail, and planning?
4. Describe a situation that did not go as well as planned. What would you have done differently?
5. Are you better at juggling a number of priorities or projects simultaneously, or attacking a few projects one at a time?
6. Everyone procrastinates at times. What are the kinds of things that you procrastinate on?

Enthusiasm

1. How would you rate yourself (and why) in enthusiasm and charisma?
2. Describe the pace at which you work—fast, slow or moderate—and the circumstances under which it varies.

Tenacity

1. What are examples of the biggest challenges you have faced and overcome?
2. What will references say is your general level of urgency?

Conflict Management

1. Describe a situation in which you actively tore down walls or barriers to teamwork.
2. If two subordinates are fighting, what do you do?
3. Describe situations in which you prevented or resolved conflicts.

Judgment/Decision Making

1. What are a couple of the most difficult or challenging decisions you have made recently?
2. What are a couple of the best and worst decisions you have made in the past year?
3. What maxims do you live by?
4. Please describe your decision-making approach when you are faced with difficult situations, in comparison with others, at about your level in the organization. Are you decisive and quick, but sometimes too quick, or are you more thorough but sometimes too slow? Are you intuitive or go purely with the facts? Do you involve many or few people in decisions?

Analysis Skills

1. Please describe your problem analysis skills.
2. What will references indicate are your style and overall effectiveness in "sorting the wheat from the chaff"?
3. What analytic approaches and tools do you use?
4. Do people generally regard you as one who diligently pursues every detail or do you tend to be more broad brush? Why?

Strategic Skills

1. In the past year, what specifically have you done in order to remain knowledgeable about the competitive environment, market dynamics, service trends, innovations, and patterns of customer behavior?
2. Please describe your experience in strategic planning, including successful and unsuccessful approaches.
3. Where do you predict (your area) is going in the next three years? What is the "conventional wisdom," and what are your own thoughts?

Risk Taking

1. What are the biggest risks you have taken in recent years? Include ones that have worked out well and not so well.

Leading Edge

1. How have you copied, created, or applied best practice?
2. Describe projects in which your best-practice solutions did and did not fully address customer needs.
3. How computer literate are you?

Political Savvy

1. Describe a couple of the most difficult, challenging, or frustrating political situations you have faced.
2. How aware are you of political forces that may affect your performance?

Persuasion

1. Describe a situation in which you were the most effective in selling an idea or yourself.
2. Describe situations in which your persuasion skills proved ineffective.

Likability

1. When were you so frustrated you did not treat someone with respect?
2. How would you describe your sense of humor?
3. Tell me about a situation in which you were expected to work with a person you disliked.

Team Player

1. What will reference checks disclose to be the common perception among peers regarding how much of a team player you are (working cooperatively, building others' confidence and self-esteem)?
2. Describe the most difficult person with whom you have had to work.
3. When have you stood up to a boss?
4. Tell me about a situation in which you felt others were wrong and you were right.

Assertiveness

1. How would you describe your level of assertiveness?
2. When there is a difference of opinion, do you tend to confront people directly, indirectly, or tend to let the situation resolve itself?
3. Please give a couple of recent specific examples in which you were highly assertive, one in which the outcome was favorable, and one where it wasn't.

Communication Skills

1. How do you communicate with your organization?
2. Describe the last time you put your "foot in your mouth"?
3. Can you tell me about a time you had to communicate an unpopular decision to an individual or group? Describe your approach and the outcome.
4. How would you rate yourself in public speaking?

Collaboration

1. Describe a successful collaborative effort that you have initiated (ask for details, such as people involved, issues raised and addressed, outcome).
2. Describe a collaborative effort that was not as successful as you had hoped. Tell me what you might have done differently to affect the outcome.
3. Can you give me an example when you were able to get very disparate groups to collaborate? (Again, ask for details, why were the groups disparate, what challenges were you able to overcome and how, etc.)

Team Building

1. Which of the teams that you have established has been the best and why? What did the team achieve?
2. Tell me about a team you built that seemed to have the right players, but just couldn't seem to accomplish its goals. Why and what did you do about it?
3. How do you get people who do not want to work together to establish a common approach to a problem?

Change Leadership

1. Tell me about a situation in which you were effective in facilitating change with an individual and with a group.
2. Describe a situation in which your attempts to facilitate change were unsuccessful. What were the most significant learnings you took away from the experience?

Creativity

1. What have you done that you consider truly creative?
2. What kinds of problems have people recently called on you to solve? Tell me what you have devised.
3. Do you consider yourself a better visionary or implementer and why?

Management Competencies

1. How would subordinates you have had in recent years describe your approaches to developing them? (Look for coaching, challenging assignments)
2. How do you go about establishing goals for performance (bottom up, top down, or what…and are they easy or "stretch")?
3. How are your expectations communicated?
4. How "ands-on" a manager are you? (Get specifics)

Process Improvement

1. Tell me about a process improvement initiative in which you took the lead, and describe the approach, the challenge, and the outcome.
2. Describe an effort to improve a process that was not as successful as you had hoped? Why was it not successful, and what might you have done differently?
3. Do people generally regard you as one who diligently pursues every detail or do you tend to be more broad brush? Why?
4. Are you better at initiating a lot of things or hammering out results for fewer things? (Get specifics)

Ambition

1. Who have been recent career influences and why?

Balance in Life

1. How satisfied are you with your balance in life—the balance among work, wellness, community involvement, professional associates, hobbies, etc.?

Energy

1. How many hours per week have you worked on the average, during the past year?
2. What motivates you?

Integrity

1. Describe a situation or two in which the pressures to compromise your integrity were the strongest you have ever felt.
2. What are a couple of the most courageous actions or unpopular stands you have ever taken?

3. When have you been confronted unethical behavior or chosen to not say anything, in order to not rock the boat?
4. Under what circumstances have you found it justifiable to break a confidence?

Intelligence

1. Please describe your learning ability.
2. Describe a complex situation in which you had to learn a lot, quickly. How did you go about learning how successful were the outcomes?

Conceptual Ability

1. Are you more comfortable dealing with concrete, tangible, or short-term or more abstract, conceptual, long-term issues? Please explain.

Pragmatism

1. Do you consider yourself a more visionary or more pragmatic thinker and why?

Appendix 7
Compliance with Equal Employment Opportunity Regulations
and Anti-Discriminatory Practices In Interviewing

Many organizations, including state equal employment opportunity agencies, offer guidelines for hiring managers, search committees, and human resources practitioners. The following are general rules and suggestions for collecting information from applicants while ensuring compliance with anti-discrimination laws and regulations. These guidelines are not complete definitions of what can and cannot be asked of applicants. When in doubt about particulars, refer to your institution's general counsel or human resources office.

The one simple rule for interview questions: Ask only questions that pertain to the position and its defined work—not questions about the applicant.

If you want to know about family constraints:

- DO ASK: What is your ability to work evenings, weekends, or additional time; do you understand that the position requires ___ % travel?
- DON'T ASK: Do you have children or family commitments that will prevent you from working long hours, traveling, or attending compulsory events?

If you are concerned about an obvious or assumed disability:

- DO ASK: Are you able to perform all the required duties of this position, with or without accommodation?
- DON'T ASK: Are you disabled? How does it affect your life? What is your prognosis?

If you want to know the candidate's age:

- DO ASK: Are you at least 18 years of age?
- DON'T ASK: How old are you? What is your date of birth? (And do not require or request birth certificates, naturalization papers, or baptismal records!)

If you want to question criminal records:

- DO ASK: Are there any arrests or convictions I should know about that are directly relevant to your job? (for example, DUI convictions if the candidate will be driving as part of her or his job duties)
- DON'T ASK: Have you ever been arrested or convicted of a felony or misdemeanor? How many times, and for what offenses?

If you want information about organizational memberships or affiliations:

- DO ASK: To which professional organizations, trade unions, or service groups do you belong that you feel are related to this position?
- DON'T ASK: Are you a member of NOW, NAACP (or any organization that might indicate racial, ethnic, gender, or ancestry affiliation)?

Remember: There are no appropriate questions you may ask pertaining to the applicant's birthplace, residence, national origin, ancestry, gender, financial status, or height and weight (unless there is a bona fide physical requirement of the job duties).

A reminder for the administrative coordinator of the search

The following situations should be handled by your human resources, general counsel, or faculty affairs offices:

- There is no reason for you to obtain a photograph until and unless your organization's personnel records require it for identification purposes upon hire. If a photograph is included in the application materials, it should not be distributed to committee members.
- You should not request or require personal references that indicate familial ancestry, religious affiliation, or citizenship. If such are included, they should not be distributed.
- It is permissible to ask whether a candidate has a family member working in the organization, particularly if the organization has a particular policy on nepotism or reporting relationships; it is permissible to ask for a relative's name, home address and other contact information only for the purpose of emergency contact information.

Appendix 8
Lehigh Valley Health Network
Leadership Competencies

Lehigh Valley Health Network developed a customized list of competencies that the organization deemed were essential at various levels of leadership. While examples of Lehigh Valley's competencies are included below as illustrative, leadership competencies would need to be tailored to an organization's particular setting, culture, mission, goals, and needs.

Domain	Competency
Strategic skills	Business acumen
	Decision quality
	Intellectual horsepower
	Learning on the fly
	Problem solving
	Dealing with ambiguity
	Creativity
	Innovation management
	Perspective
	Strategic agility
Operating skills	Priority setting
	Organizing
	Developing direct reports and others
	Process management
Courage	Command skills
	Sizing up people
Energy and drive	Drive for results
Organizational and positioning skills	Political savvy
	Presentation skills
	Comfort around higher management
Personal and interpersonal skills	Customer focus
	Managing diversity
	Motivating others
	Negotiating
	Managing vision and purpose
	Ethics and values
	Integrity and trust
	Composure
	Personal learning

Appendix 9
Northeastern Ohio Universities Colleges of Medicine and Pharmacy
Department Chair CV Evaluation

Applicant Name: _____

Reviewer Name: _____

Date of Review: _____

Please identify on a scale of 1 to 5 (1 being the lowest and 5 being the highest) the candidate's qualifications. Please add comments where appropriate.

Qualifications	Rating (1-5)
Level of education and training *Comments:*	
Record of accomplishment in scholarly activities and education *Comments:*	
Evidence of progressive leadership roles in academic administration *Comments:*	

Please identify on a scale of 1 to 5 (1 being the lowest and 5 being the highest) the candidate's experiences. Please add comments where appropriate.

Experiences	Rating (1-5)
Experience leading a department or other academic administrative area *Comments:*	
Experience in developing research areas *Comments:*	

Please identify on a scale of 1 to 5 (1 being the lowest and 5 being the highest) the candidate's experiences. Please add comments where appropriate.

Experiences	Rating (1-5)
Record of accomplishments in medical and/or graduate student teaching as well as in medical and/or graduate education development including continuing medical education *Comments:*	
Record of success in externally funded research *Comments:*	
Record of accomplishment in research and scholarly presentations and publications *Comments:*	
Experience working collaboratively with other universities, hospitals and/or health departments *Comments:*	
Experience in faculty and staff development especially helping other faculty develop their research and scholarship *Comments:*	
Vision for the future of the department *Comments:*	

Other Comments:

Appendix 10
University of Arizona College of Medicine
Department Head Candidate Evaluation Form

Candidate Name: _____

Interviewer Name: _____

Date: _____

Please rank the candidate NIH-style from 1 (best) to 5 (worst) for each of the following questions. Additional written comments are welcome.

Score

1. Does the candidate have outstanding academic qualifications? ☐

2. Does the candidate have a successful track record of faculty recruitment, retention, and development? Does the candidate understand human resource issues? ☐

3. Does the candidate subscribe to a [desired approach to discipline]? Will the candidate make development of the department along these lines a priority issue? ☐

4. Does the candidate grasp the scope and challenges of developing and managing a department spanning campuses in Phoenix and Tucson? Does the candidate recognize the opportunities presented by the college of medicine expansion in Phoenix? ☐

5. Would enhancement of the department's research profile be a major priority for the candidate? ☐

6. Would the department's NIH ranking improve under the candidate's leadership? ☐

7. Would the candidate manage a financially viable department? ☐

Score

8. Would the candidate successfully balance departmental and institutional priorities? ☐

9. Is the candidate visionary? Does the candidate articulate this vision well? ☐

10. Is the candidate a good listener? Is the candidate a good communicator? Is the candidate self-aware and adaptive? ☐

11. Having reviewed the job description and interviewed the candidate, do you feel the candidate is qualified for the position? ☐

12. Would this candidate be an advocate for the department at all levels of institutional administration? ☐

13. Does the candidate understand management of hospital relations as they relate to [department function]? ☐

14. Would this candidate emphasize excellence in resident teaching? Medical student education? Graduate student education? ☐

15. Would you like to see the candidate as our department head of [department]? ☐

16. Please rate the candidate A, B, or C and describe areas of strength and weakness. ☐

Northeastern Ohio Universities College of Medicine
Interview Evaluation

Applicant Name: _____   **Date of Interview:** _____

Position: _____   **Reviewer(s) Name:** _____

Please evaluate the candidate below as soon as possible after the interview by circling a number on the scale, which best expresses your judgment (10=high, 1=low). Feel free to add comments below or on the reverse side. Evaluations should be directly related to the position above.

1. Applicant level of educational/professional   1 2 3 4 5 6 7 8 9 10
   background

   _____

2. Level of related work experience   1 2 3 4 5 6 7 8 9 10

   _____

3. Supervisory experience   1 2 3 4 5 6 7 8 9 10

   _____

4. Growth/leadership ability   1 2 3 4 5 6 7 8 9 10

   _____

5. Self-presentation   1 2 3 4 5 6 7 8 9 10
   (include confidence, appearance, ability to
   represent NEOUCOM)

   _____

6. Attitude   1 2 3 4 5 6 7 8 9 10
   (include interest, enthusiasm, passion for
   [discipline, area of focus])

   _____

7. Communication skills   1 2 3 4 5 6 7 8 9 10

Additional questions to consider:

1. Candidate's strengths:

   _____

2. Candidate's weakness:

   _____

3. Did the candidate answer all questions to your satisfaction? If not, which questions were left unanswered?

   _____

4. Does the candidate understand the opportunities and challenges involved in leading [specify department/unit particulars]?

   _____

5. Did the candidate effectively communicate a vision for the [department]?

   _____

7. Do you have any reservations about this candidate's ability to succeed as chair?

   _____

Overall rating: 1   2   3   4   5   6   7   8   9   10

Would you recommend the candidate for this position?

Yes_____   No_____

If not, reason: _____

_____

_____

_____

Template of Appointment Letter

Date _____

Faculty Member Name, M.D. _____
Rank, Department of _____
Title _____
School Name _____
City, State _____ Zip _____

Dear Dr. _____:

We are most pleased to offer you the position of _____ of the department of
_____ at ABC College of Medicine of XYZ University [, and appointment as
the director of (_____), with an effective date of _____].

1. XYZ University Appointment

Your appointment is to the faculty as (RANK) of (DEPT NAME) in the college of
medicine. ABC College of Medicine is dedicated to developing and maintaining a
strong commitment to ethical teaching practices at all levels of the education process.
As a member of the faculty, you are expected to uphold the tenets of the Educator's
Code of Conduct (Appendix I).

[Describe nature of appointment and tenure. E.g., for senior faculty: This is a
standing, tenure-eligible position. Application for immediate tenure will be made
prior to your arrival. The dean of the college of medicine supports the application
for immediate tenure for your appointment in the college of medicine. As this
process involves the college and university tenure committees, the actual award of
tenure may occur following your arrival on campus. Your appointment as a professor
of _____ is subject to university and college policies regarding faculty
appointments.]

2. ABC College of Medicine Appointment

Your clinical appointment, including any administrative and service responsibilities,
at ABC Medical Center and related practice sites will be as (RANK) of (DEPT
NAME). Clinical faculty and medical directors serve at the discretion of the executive
director and chief operating officer (COO) of the Penn State Milton S. Hershey
Medical Center, with the concurrence of the chair, and are subject to removal with or
without cause.

[3. The Administrative Appointment

[You also will be appointed to the administrative position of _____. As with
all administrative positions, you serve at the discretion of the dean of the college of
medicine, and are subject to removal with or without cause. However, removal from
this administrative position would not affect your status as a tenure-eligible or
tenured _____.]

4. Effort, Compensation, Incentives, and Benefits

Your compensation, as is the case with all clinical faculty members, will be paid through ABC Medical Center. Our organization is values-based, performance driven, and strategy focused. As such, we strive for an equitable distribution of resources, responsibilities, and rewards. Our strategic plan (Appendix II) offers more detail about our values, guiding principles, and strategy for the future.

A. Effort, Base Salary and Incentive Compensation

- Your expected allocation of effort is ____% academic, ___% research, __ % service/administration, and ___% in the direct care of patients.

- Your academic appointment to the ABC College of Medicine is separate from your employment. The academic appointment is for 48 weeks per year in accord with XYZ University policy.

- An ongoing analysis of faculty effort allocation by mission and its relationship to salaries is in place at the institutional level. As a consequence, we have implemented an effort-based faculty salary program within all departments that strives to set base compensations at the median for rank and performance and the AAMC Salary Survey 75th percentile and above for productivity.

- Your base salary at appointment and for the fiscal year beginning is $_____ per annum.

- You will be eligible to participate in our departmental incentive plan at completion of your first fiscal year. Your incentive payment will depend on the performance of the department, the medical center, your successful leadership, and development as a productive faculty member in accordance to a plan that we will mutual devise during your first year.

- Your salary after your first fiscal year will be eligible for evaluation and possible adjustment.

- You also are eligible to receive payments under our research incentive plan (Appendix III – *Academic Compensation Plan*).

- You will receive a salary stipend of $XXX for your [administrative appointment]. If your [administrative appointment] is discontinued by action of the college of medicine, your compensation for a period of one year thereafter will be at your specified base salary. Beyond that period, your salary will be as determined by the _____and the dean as appropriate for a _____.

B. Benefits

- Summaries of the retirement and health benefits for ABC Medical Center are attached. Our retirement plan requires a five-year vesting period for the employer contribution portion of your retirement plan. You will be appointed on a full-time basis with 10 holidays each year.

- [CME reimbursement—as appropriate]

- [Journal subscriptions—as appropriate]

- [Computers and technical administrative support—as appropriate]

- Please understand that you are entitled to these employee benefits that are currently in effect or as amended from time to time, as applicable.

5. Relocation Expenses

Our policy on reimbursement of moving costs is a maximum of ($X,000) for moving your personal property to the ABC area (Appendix IV). Any incurred costs greater than this amount must be pre-approved on an exception-basis by the chief financial officer. Please contact Jane Doe in our Medical Center Purchasing Department to make arrangements with our contracted moving companies.

Please review the relocation policies for the approved expenses for visits prior to your start date, housing and accommodations, and travel expenses, and spousal travel limitations.

6. Mutual Commitments and Expectations

The position requires a full-time commitment. It is expected that you will spend your time carrying out leadership and administrative duties as in a manner to enhance high-quality clinical services, promote excellence in education and training programs, and establish and expand research.

It is the expectation that all faculty members commit to the mission and values of the college of medicine and medical center. These values of respect, trust, teamwork, collaboration, and excellence are the enduring tenets that guide what we do in both our long-term strategies and our day-today interactions. We are expecting that you will foster a positive milieu by demonstrating and reflecting these values. The *Physician's Commitment to Care* (Appendix V) document offers explicit information about this commitment.

The culture of the college of medicine and medical center is predicated upon teamwork in the belief that we are stronger working as a team than as a collective of individual or departmental pursuits. Both risks and gains are shared across the institution as we strive for collective success in the pursuit of excellence in everything we do.

Faculty members may be asked to participate as team members of high profile departmental or institutional committees or teams. Your assignment would be based on a mutual discussion in alignment with your areas of expertise, interest, capacity, and career aspirations.

7. Performance Evaluations, Career Development, and Mentoring

As with all clinical faculty members, you will receive an annual performance review by [supervisor]. The review will include an evaluation of your performance by mission, and will focus on collaborative and constructive planning for the future. Each review will include your written annual report and will involve thorough one-on-one discussions with [administrative officer] about your teaching, research, service, future plans, assignments, and salary.

Annual performance review is not only necessary for the process of determining merit salary increases; it also provides an occasion for self-evaluation and reassessment of the role a faculty member is playing, which may evolve significantly during the course of a career. The review process offers an opportunity to acknowledge and recognize good work, point out areas for improvement, and, identify productive new uses of a faculty member's talents. It is a means of ensuring that the diverse talents of the entire faculty are productively applied to the many responsibilities of the university. In addition, performance reviews can help identify faculty development targets. At the college of medicine and medical center, every annual performance review includes a development plan for the individual faculty member.

Faculty development opportunities may involve leadership training at the Institute for Faculty Leadership Development, enrollment in the Junior Faculty Development Program, establishment of mentoring relationships with other faculty members, or specific development opportunities outside of the organization such as the Josiah Macy Scholars or Robert Wood Johnson Scholars programs. *Evaluation of Faculty Performance* is included as Appendix VI.

8. Institutional Philosophy and Values

Appendix II is explicit in describing our organization as values based. Respect, trust, collegiality and collaboration, and the constant pursuit of excellence are not only the values that guide us, but are hallmarks of the work of the organization. In order to be certain that we remain "on target," patient and employee satisfaction are measured at regular intervals. Likewise, organizational and individual performance measures are integral to ascertain that the organization is making best use of precious resources as we strive for an equitable distribution of resources, responsibilities, and rewards.

9. Mission of the Department

The mission of the department of (DEPT NAME) is to develop superlative educational, clinical, and research programs that will establish the department as a top tier department, as well as the preferred referral service in central Pennsylvania. The department of (DEPT NAME) is committed to a values-based approach for achieving these missions. As for the institution as a whole, the values of respect, trust, teamwork and collaboration, and excellence guide the work of the department. As a key faculty member of the department of (DEPT NAME), you will be responsible for fostering a departmental environment that reflects these values.

Departmental Goals
The departmental goals, which are in alignment with the overall campus strategic goals, include the following:

- [DEPT Goal #1]

- [DEPT Goal #2]

- [DEPT Goal #3]

- The department works closely with the office of medical education to ensure high quality in educational experiences for our medical students. (DELINEATE TEACHING EXPECTATIONS)

10. Personnel Support

An operations director and senior administrator are assigned to the department of (DEPT NAME). The administrator provides support to the operations director in (DEPT NAME) and a limited number of other departments. The chair, operations director, and administrator work together to appropriately staff the department and ensure smooth operations across the academic, clinical, and research missions.

Research support services are available to you through the office of the vice dean for research and graduate studies to focus efforts on securing extramural funding for the full scope of research. Recruitment of postdoctoral scholars or fellows will be based upon the needs and resources of funded investigators within the department.

11. Financial & Space Commitments

We are vigilant stewards of our precious resources that occur in the form of space, people, finances and time. Performance standards have been established for many of the institutional processes used to sustain and replenish organizational resources. Redesign efforts are underway in several areas including the revenue cycle, supply chain, and allocation of space and capital equipment.

Research Support
In addition to the funds described above, the college of medicine provides research support and start-up costs related to the hiring of new faculty. Joint academic appointments also will be used to promote collaborative research across departments.

The award of initial start-up funds is driven by the status of the investigator at the time of recruitment and the application of the *Academic Compensation Plan.* The college of medicine has budgeted $_____ as a three-year start-up package for you to successfully establish a laboratory on campus. As described in the college of medicine *Academic Compensation Plan* (Appendix III), you are expected to cover costs at the end of this start-up period.

Capital Equipment
You and I will work together to identify specific pieces of equipment to be acquired for your specific research [OR your specific area of clinical expertise]. Equipment purchases are evaluated and prioritized during the annual capital budget process and five-year capital plan to ensure that we are using this budget to maximize overall institutional performance while meeting departmental needs.

Laboratory and Office Space
Your laboratory and office space will be provided for resident research, new researchers, and for your own research in the department of (DEPT NAME), room _____, amounting to [___] square feet. Laboratory space is based on the amount of funded research in the department in accord with the benchmarks and process established by the Physical Resources Team, with oversight by the associate dean for research.

12. Performance of Services

In accepting this appointment, you agree to not engage in the performance of services on behalf of any other organization and you will practice medicine only as an employee of the AMC Medical Center, unless the chair and dean or executive director/COO approves an exception in writing.

13. Patents, Discoveries, Inventions, Copyrightable Works, Intellectual Property

In accepting this appointment, you agree to abide by the policies and regulations in force during your employment with respect to the ownership and patenting of discoveries, inventions and other intellectual property, and the ownership of copyrightable works. (Appendix XXXX)

14. Restricted Covenant and Non-Competition for Clinical Activities

Please understand that your position requires a restrictive covenant that is necessitated because of the time and resources associated with your recruitment costs, the considerable efforts that have been devoted by other medical center faculty physicians and personnel in assisting you in the development and maintenance of your clinical practice, and the additional time and effort that would be required to continue the practice that you would be leaving in the future.

Therefore, acceptance of this position constitutes your understanding and agreement to restrict your practice of medicine, in the event that your employment terminates, to an area outside of the service area of the ABC Medical Center following such termination. This restriction shall endure for two (2) years from the date of termination, and shall apply regardless of the reason for the termination, whether initiated for reasons of your own or the employer. This restriction applies not only to any office you may seek to establish within the restricted area for my practice, but to staff memberships and the exercise of clinical privileges at any health care facility located in the restricted area.

15. Conflicts of Interest Disclosure and Resolution Process

Conflicts of interest may take various forms. A conflict of interest (COI) exists if a significant financial interest or other opportunities for tangible personal benefit may exert a substantial and improper influence upon a faculty member. A conflict of interest may exist when there is a divergence between the private interests of a faculty member and the faculty member's obligation to research participants, patients, or to the organization. All faculty members must make an annual disclosure of real or perceived conflicts of interest. In some cases, a plan for eliminating, reducing, or managing the conflict of interest involving the faculty member. XYZ University Policy and the ABC College of Medicine Conflict of Interest Policies are attached as Appendix VII, parts a and b.

16. Appointment Termination

 Your appointment may be terminated by either you or the employer (a) for cause upon prior written notice of at least ten days, or (b) without cause upon prior written notice of at least 90 days.

✶ ✶ ✶ ✶ ✶

In conclusion, we would like to emphasize that we believe this plan puts you in a position to impact the department's future. We are excited by the potential of your leadership. We are confident that you will add to the development of a nationally recognized department at ABC College of Medicine. To indicate your commitment to this agreement, please sign below and return the signed original to us.

Sincerely,
Chair's Name, MD
Dean's Name, MD

Appendix 13
University of Arizona College of Medicine
Candidate Visit Feedback Form

Thank you for visiting the University of Arizona College of Medicine! In an effort to improve candidate visits, we ask that you fill out the evaluation form below regarding your recent visit.

EVALUATION

Using a scale of 1 (strongly agree) to 5 (strongly disagree), please answer the questions below:

	1	2	3	4	5
	Strongly agree			Strongly disagree	
1 The accommodations were to my satisfaction.	1	2	3	4	5
2 Travel was taken care of in a timely manner.	1	2	3	4	5
3 I was appropriately escorted to appointments.	1	2	3	4	5
4 The length of appointments was appropriate.	1	2	3	4	5
5 The number of appointments was appropriate.	1	2	3	4	5
6 Appointments were scheduled with the right people, e.g., the people I needed to see.	1	2	3	4	5
7 The arrangements for my talk were handled well.	1	2	3	4	5
8 I felt welcomed at the college of medicine.	1	2	3	4	5

Please provide any other comments on how we could have improved your visit:

References

AAMC. Women in U.S. academic medicine statistics and medical school benchmarking, 2007–2008. Available at http://www.aamc.org/members/gwims/statistics/stats08/start.htm. Accessed September 30, 2009.

American Council on Education. *The American College President.* Washington, D.C.: American Council on Education, 2002.

Banaji MR, Bazerman MH, Chugh D. How (un)ethical are you? *Harv Bus Rev.* 2003;81:56–64.

Bennis W, O'Toole J. Don't hire the wrong CEO. *Harv Bus Rev.* 2000;78(3):170–176,218.

Bertrand M, Mullainathan S. Are Emily and Greg more employable than Lakisha and Jamal? A field experiment on labor market discrimination. May 27, 2003. MIT Department of Economics Working Paper No. 03-22. http://ssrn.com/abstract=422902. Accessed September 30, 2009.

Biebuyck JF, Mallon WT. *The Successful Medical School Department Chair: Search, Selection, Appointment, Transition.* Washington, D.C.: AAMC; 2002.

Biebuyck JF, Mallon WT. *The Successful Medical School Department Chair: Characteristics, Responsibilities, Expectation, Skill Sets.* Washington, D.C.: AAMC; 2003.

Biernat M, Manis M. Shifting standards and stereotype-based judgments. *Journal of Personality and Social Psychology.* 1994;66:5–20.

Bland CJ, Ruffin MT. Characteristics of a productive research environment: Literature review. *Acad Med* 67;1992: 385-397.

Bradberry T. *Squawk!* New York: Collins Business; 2008.

Corrice A. Unconscious bias in faculty and leadership recruitment: A literature review. *AAMC Analysis in Brief.* August, 2009.

Creasman WT. Is this any way to choose a chair? *Acad Med.* 2001;76:1032–1034.

Dohrenwend A. Perspective: A grand challenge to academic medicine: Speak out on gay rights. *Acad Med.* 2009;84:788–792.

Fernández-Aráoz C, Groysberg B, Nohria N. The definitive guide to recruiting in good times and bad. *Harv Bus Rev* [serial online]. May 1, 2009.

Garrison SA. *Institutional Search: A Practical Guide to Executive Recruitment in Nonprofit Organizations.* New York: Praeger; 1989.

Goldin C, Rouse C. Orchestrating impartiality: The impact of "blind" auditions on female musicians. *Am Econ Rev.* 2000;90:715–741.

Gilmore TN. *Finding and Retaining Your Next Chief Executive: Making the Transition Work.* Washington, D.C.: National Center for Nonprofit Boards; 1993.

Graves LM. College recruitment: Removing personal bias from selection decisions. *Personnel.* 1989;66:48–52.

Grigsby RK, Hefner DS, Souba WW, Kirch DG. The future-oriented department chair. *Acad Med.* 2004;79:571–577.

Heilman ME, Okimoto TG. Why are women penalized for success at male tasks?: The implied communality deficit. *Journal of Applied Psychology.* 2007;92:81–92.

Hochel S, Wilson CE. *Hiring Right: Conducting Successful Searches in Higher Education.* San Francisco, CA: Jossey-Bass Publishers; 2007.

Hoffmeir PA. Are search committees really searching? *Acad Med.* 2003;78:125–128.

Kennedy J. Behavior-based interviewing: Does it still work? *The HR Bulletin* [serial online]. March, 2001.

King EB, Madera JM, Hebl MR, Knight JL, Mendoza SA. What's in a name? A multiracial investigation of the role of occupational stereotypes in selection decisions. *J Appl Soc Psychol.* 2006;36:1145–1159.

Mahoney FE. Adjusting the interview to avoid cultural bias. *J Career Plan Employ.* 1992;52:41–43.

Mahoney MR, Wilson E, Odom KL, Flowers L, Adler SR. Minority faculty voices on diversity in academic medicine: Perspectives from one school. *Acad Med.* 2008; 83:781-786.

Mallon WT, Corrice A. *Leadership Recruiting Practices in U.S. Medical Schools: How Medical Schools Search for New Department Chairs and Center Directors.* Washington, D.C.: AAMC; 2009.

Marchese TJ, Lawrence JF. *The Search Committee Handbook: A Guide to Recruiting Administrators.* 2nd ed. Sterling, Va.: Stylus; 2006.

Martell RF. Sex bias at work: The effects of attentional and memory demands on performance ratings of men and women. *J Appl Soc Psychol.* 1991;21:1939–1960.

McLaughlin JB. Plugging search committee leaks. *AGB Reports.* 1985:May/June;24–30.

McLaughlin JB. The pros and cons of using headhunters. In: Stein RH, Trachtenberg SJ, eds. *The Art of Hiring in America's Colleges and Universities.* Buffalo, N.Y.: Prometheus Books; 1993:155–168.

McLaughlin JB, Riesman D. *Choosing a College President: Opportunities and Constraints.* Princeton, N.J.: Carnegie Foundation for the Advancement of Teaching; 1990.

Nosek BA, Banaji MR, Greenwald AG. Harvesting implicit group attitudes and beliefs from a demonstration web site. *Group Dyn.* 2002;6:101–115.

Quillen DA, Aber RC, Grigsby RK. Interim department chairs in academic medicine. *Am J Med.* In press.

Schein EH. *Organizational Culture and Leadership.* 3rd ed. San Francisco: Jossey-Bass Publishers; 2004.

Sessa VI, Kaiser R, Taylor JK, Campbell RJ. *Executive Selection: A Research Report on What Works and What Doesn't.* Greensboro, N.C.: Center for Creative Leadership; 1998.

Sessa VI, Taylor JJ. *Executive Selection: Strategies for Success.* San Francisco: Jossey-Bass Publishers; 2000.

Souba WW, McFadden DW. The double whammy of change. *J Surg Res.* 2009;151:1–5.

Stein RH, Trachtenberg SJ. *The Art of Hiring in America's Colleges and Universities.* Buffalo, N.Y.: Prometheus Books; 1993.

Steinpres RE, Anders KA, Ritzke D. The impact of gender on the review of the curricula vitae of job applicants and tenure candidates: A national empirical study. *Sex Roles.* 1999;41:509–528.

Touchton JG. Maybe you need a search firm? *AAHE Bulletin.* 1989;42(4):6–9.

Trix F, Psenka C. Exploring the color of glass: Letters of recommendation for female and male medical faculty. *Discourse & Society.* 2003;14:191–220.

Valian V. Recruitment and retention: Guidelines for chairs, heads, and deans. 2008. Available at http://www.hunter.cuny.edu/genderequity/equityMaterials/Feb2008/recruitretain.pdf. Accessed September 30, 2009.

Van Buren ME, Safferstone T. The quick wins paradox. *Harv Bus Rev.* 2009;87(1):55–61.

Vicker LA, Royer HJ. *The Complete Academic Search Manual: A Systematic Approach to Successful and Inclusive Hiring.* Sterling, Va.: Stylus; 2005.

Wennerås C, Wold A. Nepotism and sexism in peer-review. *Nature.* 1997;387:341–343.

Will KH. Mind the gap. *Chron High Educ* [serial online]. July 6, 2009.

About the Authors

William T. Mallon, Ed.D., is senior director, organizational learning and research, at the AAMC, where he leads research and programming on faculty work life, organizational studies, and leadership in academic medicine. He is the author of 35 journal articles, book chapters, and monographs; his studies have appeared in journals such as *Science, Academic Medicine, Innovative Higher Education,* and *New Directions in Higher Education.* He is author of *The Handbook of Academic Medicine: How Medical Schools and Teaching Hospitals Work* (2009), *Tenure on Trial: Case Studies of Change in Faculty Employment Policies* (2001), and coauthor of *The Successful Medical School Department Chair* series (2002-03). He was educated at the University of Richmond and Harvard University.

R. Kevin Grigsby, M.S.W., D.S.W., is senior director, organizational leadership and development, at the AAMC. Prior to his arrival at the AAMC, he served as vice dean for faculty and administrative affairs and professor in the department of psychiatry at Pennsylvania State University College of Medicine. He has an extensive history of program planning, implementation, and evaluation in the area of innovative home and community-based health and mental health services. During the past decade, the focus of his work has shifted to organizational development in academic health centers. He remains active in promoting effective interpersonal communication within academic health centers and in implementing alternative conflict resolution/management strategies at the department and institutional levels. He has been instrumental in developing career development programs and is an Editorial Advisory Board member and frequent contributor to *Academic Physician and Scientist.*

Mary Dupont Barrett served as associate dean for human resources at Harvard Medical School from 1999 through 2008 and as director of human resources from 1996 to 2008. She is a founding member of the AAMC's Human Resources Forum and is a consultant to the Group on Business Affairs, working to encourage and enhance the contribution of HR professionals to the body of knowledge crucial to AAMC's member institutions. She currently works with academic institutions and other nonprofit organizations to align and integrate human resource policies, practices, and processes. She earned a bachelor's degree in organizational development and a master's degree in labor relations and research from the University of Massachusetts at Amherst.